EMPLOYEE-CENTRIC IT

ADVANCING THE DIGITAL ERA THROUGH EXTRAORDINARY IT EXPERIENCE

Mark Ghibril

Apress®

Employee-Centric IT: Advancing the Digital Era Through Extraordinary IT Experience

Mark Ghibril
Pamplona, Spain

ISBN-13 (pbk): 978-1-4842-9185-6   ISBN-13 (electronic): 978-1-4842-9186-3
https://doi.org/10.1007/978-1-4842-9186-3

Copyright © 2023 by Mark Ghibril

Managing Director, Apress Media LLC: Welmoed Spahr
Acquisitions Editor: Shiva Ramachandran
Development Editor: James Markham
Coordinating Editor: Jessica Vakili

Distributed to the book trade worldwide by Springer Science+Business Media New York, 1 New York Plaza, New York, NY 10004. Phone 1-800-SPRINGER, fax (201) 348-4505, e-mail orders-ny@springer-sbm.com, or visit www.springeronline.com. Apress Media, LLC is a California LLC and the sole member (owner) is Springer Science + Business Media Finance Inc (SSBM Finance Inc). SSBM Finance Inc is a **Delaware** corporation.

For information on translations, please e-mail booktranslations@springernature.com; for reprint, paperback, or audio rights, please e-mail bookpermissions@springernature.com.

Apress titles may be purchased in bulk for academic, corporate, or promotional use. eBook versions and licenses are also available for most titles. For more information, reference our Print and eBook Bulk Sales web page at http://www.apress.com/bulk-sales.

Printed on acid-free paper

To my wife Vicki, whose clear view that an IT book will make her fall asleep faster made me work harder to make it less boring!

To my daughter Monroe, who told me she will read it one day when she is old!

To my daughter Stella, whose birth date pushed me to finish the book on time!

To every IT employee and leader I had the pleasure and honor to work and shape this topic with: I hope I did all our efforts justice!

Contents

About the Author

Mark Ghibril is a senior executive with global leadership experience in business digital transformation, strategy, operations, and cyber security. Mark works alongside C-suite peers to drive business value and business change through advice on and implementation of enterprise-wide digital tools and integrated platforms. He has pioneered innovative employee IT experience, interaction concepts, models, and tools through a global center of excellence in user engagement and experience. Mark is a board advisor to several startups on digital automation, ecommerce technology, and customer experience, offering strategic and tactical frameworks to capitalize on their investments. Mark is passionate about technology and how it positively influences organizations and society and shares his thought leadership through his blog: www.thedigitalconsumer.org.

Introduction

Today, companies are putting colossal effort and priority on digital transformations, customer experience, and product designs as differentiation in the market; however, such effort, investment, and transformation are not seen from an employee perspective. Companies are competing for customers' attention, but they are not caring about the attention of their employees.

Companies are fighting for talent, calling it the new GOLD of the digital age. Still, no one is fighting and putting the same energy and resources into ensuring their employee's experience is the GOLD standard, maybe copper or even lower.

Research and surveys show that more than 80% of new hires decide to stay or leave a company within the first six months, and more than 60% are more likely to stay longer than three years if they have good experience from onboarding to doing their daily work. Finally, a company's cost is up to 300% of an employee's salary to replace them, and it takes approximately eight months for a newly hired employee to reach full productivity.

Research and surveys show that organizations that can enhance their employee experience reap enormous rewards from enhanced customer satisfaction, reduced churn, increased revenue, and greater employee satisfaction.

As Doug Conant, an internationally renowned business leader, bestselling author, and founder of Conant Leadership, said: To win in the marketplace, you must first win in the workplace.

A huge amount of work, research, and models is now shared to improve employee engagement, motivation, and experience. A similar amount of work and books is done on improving business stakeholders and digital transformation at the board level. Still, they haven't concentrated on a crucial aspect in this digital remote world: employee experience with their IT and digital tools.

Research has shown that more than 25% of technology projects are canceled or delivered tools that employees barely use or adopt. Global surveys from McKinsey, BCG, Gartner, and others show that less than 30% of digital transformation programs succeed in improving the company's performance and employee productivity.

Research and experience show that small organizations have much higher success rates of digital transformation than much bigger ones. In addition, more than 70% of digital transformations are usually focusing on digitalizing the organization's operations and internal processes.

All the data points to a common denominator: the employee. More than two-thirds of today's jobs require employees' good digital and IT skills. The expectations of senior management, who invest in these big digital transformations, are that the employees will become more productive and effective and help the bottom line. However, this can only happen through an active and proactive change of IT operations, transformations, and support to become employee-centric rather than today's technology-centric or senior management–centric IT.

In every organization, employees, from office workers in finance, HR, and other corporate functions to workers in the field, factories, and warehouses, rely on IT to perform their job in some way or another. Based on a persona-based activity I have conducted for several years, the average number of tools used by any employee in a day is five, with some ending up with ten.

So, it's fair that employees are usually skeptical about using new tools, frustrated with the number of tools to use, and even the way they get support. They skip or don't trust in learnings because they are long and complex or prioritize other business activities that tools don't support.

In my years of experience, I have seen the benefit of moving toward employee-centricity in IT. Employees gain more technology aptitude, are up for technology change, and are willing to learn more for their benefit and even provide feedback on improving these tools, training, and support. In addition, employee-centric IT will transform employees to own their digital literacy and development, reduce or eliminate the shadow IT needs, and allow the organization to drive and implement successful digital transformation.

So in this book, I would like to provide you with the aims and goals you should target in your IT organization to transform how you deliver IT to your employees. Based on my experience, experience of others, and research outside IT, especially in sociology, psychology, and anthropology, I will help you put the employee (the human) in the heart of everything you do in IT and what I like to call it: the employee-centric IT.

In Part 1, I will share with you why we need to move from a technology-centric IT to an employee-centric one and why employee-centric IT is a key pillar of the entire employee experience in an organization. I will also share with you the trust equation that I will use to take you through all the concepts I propose in this book.

Then, in Part 2, I will share how you can win the employees' hearts and the goals you should set yourself to engage with the employees, support them, and provide a culture they feel is concentrated on them.

In Part 3, I will reveal how you can win the employees' minds by turning your operations, transformations, and innovation toward employee-centricity.

In Part 4, I will uncover, after having now the hearts and minds of the employees, how you can also gain the trust of the management, your IT employees, and everyone else.

In Part 5, I will be putting all the steps together in a playbook to be used in implementing employee-centricity in an organization.

The chapters in Parts 2–5 will contain concepts, goals, and a checklist that contains preparation steps, problem-solving steps, and prevention steps (where it applies) to execute the concepts.

The concepts and checklists will cover steps to win the hearts of your employees and then their minds and finally to build on those to ensure trust is anchored in your IT organization as well.

This journey to employee-centric IT will just begin with this book. The ideas in this book are simply the first of many to come, and I look forward to you sharing your experiences, new ideas, and improvements with me. I am confident that the future of IT will be far away from frustrating, difficult, and confusing to the employees but rather exciting and inclusive, enabling employee engagement, motivation, and satisfaction.

The Need for Employee-Centric IT

On a sunny Monday morning, Sara woke up excited to start her career at one of the leading healthcare companies. She arrived at the office at 8:30 am for her first day. She was greeted by her manager, introduced to her colleagues, and assigned a workspace.

On the second day, she was given her initial tasks and the tools she could use. Even though Sara is a biotech engineer and technology savvy, she realized that she would need to learn the following new systems and others, some regularly, and some based on need:

- A new HR system to log hours, salary information, and holiday booking
- A travel tool for booking business trips and submitting expenses
- A collaboration portal to store department information
- An ordering tool for any additional software she might need
- A project management tool

Day after day, Sara struggled to work with all these tools. She received very little training and support, so she left her company after five months. Sara's story is not uncommon in big corporations and highlights the need to move from a technology-centric IT to an employee-centric one. Chapters 1 and 2 explore this further.

From Technology-Centric to Employee-Centric IT

In IT, we don't have the option to wait for years or centuries to get a technology or solution to be well adopted and utilized. Digital transformation is moving at lightning speeds across all organizations, and IT teams are asked to deliver on a vast number of initiatives. Delivering results quickly while driving short-term value to the business.

© Mark Ghibril 2023
M. Ghibril, *Employee-Centric IT*, https://doi.org/10.1007/978-1-4842-9186-3_1

In this first chapter, I will introduce you to the dysfunctions of IT and their common issues and how better we can understand employees as humans and not data points.

Dysfunctions of IT

In the 18th century, British sailors suffered from a disease that was worse than any enemy they faced: scurvy. In one British expedition in the Pacific Ocean in the 1740s, the British navy lost 1300 sailors out of the 2000 just from scurvy.

Scurvy's symptoms include fungous flesh, putrid gums, and immobile crew. Many different remedies were mentioned, from eating rats to malt and sauerkraut and even citrus fruits.

However, only a century later from the first documentation of the power of "sour lemons and oranges" on treating/avoiding scurvy, Dr. James Lind was able to publish a scientific literature to treat scurvy, which earned him a place in the scientific history.

In 1747, Dr. Lind carried out a clinical trial on board HMS Salisbury. He took 12 men suffering from symptoms of scurvy, divided them into six pairs, and treated them with different remedies. This clinical trial, which is one of the first ever recorded in history, proved the benefit of oranges and lemons as cure for scurvy.

Today, Dr. Lind is a hero for the Royal Navy, and the Institute of Naval Medicine's official crest adorns a lemon tree.

However, what is very interesting in this story is that scurvy outbreaks continued to affect many sailors even after Dr. Lind's treatise was circulated widely. And only in 1928 when vitamin C was identified, the scurvy disease was defeated completely. So why did the Royal Navy need almost half a century to act on his findings and why did it need another century to defeat the disease?

Researchers believe it has to do with the following reasons:

- The treatise shared was 450 pages long, and the real account on the oranges and lemons trail only took four pages out of it.

- A counter-publicist, captain cook, who the naval trusted and who was favoring malt and sauerkraut cure.

- Even when the Naval Admirals made lemon juice compulsory on ships, the methods used to preserve it (e.g., boiling the juice) destroyed the vitamin C or they used cheaper limes from the Caribbean.

This story is a perfect example of how only if we are human-centric in our thinking we will be able to effectively drive change and adoption of new technology or cures.

To date, majority of IT teams are focusing primarily on technology and are highlighting these common issues:

- Projects need to move fast but are failing to move as quickly as business wants. IT organizations are juggling many projects and driven mainly by needs of technology rather than employee-centric outcomes.

- Business and employees have a low opinion of IT as technology-driven decisions seem to reduce trust in the business. In addition, business management and employees have two different views on IT departments, especially that IT teams concentrate their collaboration and partnering on an executive level more than the employee level.

- Low morale within IT teams due to business pressures and disjointed decision-making for the benefit of the employees. Business and employees see IT primarily as a technology support function, while IT assumes many additional roles, especially as the digital transformation driver for the company.

This IT dysfunction can only be altered through a makeover of IT from a technology-centric organization to an employee-centric one.

Understanding Employees As Humans and Not Data Points

FedEx, a leader in shipping and logistics, has been breaking new ground and striving to provide best solutions in their industry from the moment they took off to the skies in 1973. While studying at Yale in the 1960s, FedEx founder Fred Smith's thesis was about a reliable system to deliver urgent, time-sensitive shipments, and ten years later, FedEx has emerged. FedEx was behind many pioneering innovations in the logistics industry such as the tracking number, handheld computers, bar codes, and PC-based automated shipping systems.

Today, FedEx has a huge fleet of airplanes, hybrid electric commercial trucks, and soon self-driving trucks. FedEx transports more than three million items to over 200 countries each day. All the technology, complexity of logistics and worldwide shipment, will not be able to deliver the package to the customer without full engagement and commitment from the 400,000 employees across the globe. FedEx's customer feedback and satisfaction is the way they have complemented technology with their employees. This is where IT is ensuring any tools delivered in FedEx and used are fully engaged with employees.

The FedEx story highlights that IT must understand employees as humans and not simple data points. Of course, HR and digital transformation is driving a huge data collection about employees. Data is crucial to drive certain actions and decisions that drive the organization forward. However, to allow employees to fully engage with the IT tools and transformation, they need to feel they have a digital experience that suffices for their mental and emotional states.

This can only be done by an employee-centric IT rather than a technology-centric one.

Summary

I hope now you are on board that employees must be the center of IT activities in this digital age to deliver successful programs and outcomes, high business and employee satisfaction and experience, and increased morale within IT teams. In the next chapter, I will define employee experience and the key pillars that make employee experience.

Employee Experience and Its Core Pillar: Employee-Centric IT

The Human Library, or "Menneskebiblioteket" as it is called in Danish, was developed in Copenhagen in the spring of 2000. In this library, instead of borrowing a book to read a story, you borrow a person.

Started as a project at a festival by four social justice advocates and friends, this project has become a global phenomenon and now exists in over 70 countries.

© Mark Ghibril 2023

M. Ghibril, *Employee-Centric IT*, https://doi.org/10.1007/978-1-4842-9186-3_2

The concept is simple: every event offers different titles, such as "Alcoholic," "Autism," "Naturism," and others, and when you choose a title, you get either an in-group or one-on-one time with a human book who shares their life stories, makes conversations and answers questions.

From the first event that saw more than 1000 people choosing titles and experiencing the transparent, personal, and empathetic discussions to now, the Human Library became a global movement to eradicate fear and hatred of different ethnicities, social statuses, and ideologies as well as developing skills such as communication, listening reflections, and many more.

The Human Library project is a great proof of the contact hypothesis theory, which was developed in the 1950s by Gordon Allport, Ph.D., and later expanded by Psychologist Professor Thomas Pettigrew of the University of California, Santa Cruz. Both Gordon and Thomas postulated that a meaningful contact could develop way better interactions and connections between people and open people's minds to accepting new and different ideas and topics.

The Human Library project is an excellent example that experience trumps engagement in relation to adapting to change, to open minds to new ideas and to drive better communications and interactions within humans.

This is also now very clear in all the research and results seen in how organizations, which have been very much preoccupied with the concept of employee engagement since the 1990s, are shifting course to employee experience instead.

This statement was put nicely by Mark Levy, who was one of the first people with the title "Global Head of Employee Experience" at Airbnb:

> Employee Experience is all about helping companies make the shift from **talking to** their employees to **talking with** their employees.

For me, employee experience is the culmination of all the interactions an employee has within their organization to achieve the right mental, emotional, and physical states that impact their performance, engagement, and satisfaction.

Employee experience is getting a huge traction in today's business world. Even though every company will need to build their own employee experience model, there has been a few models that provide solid foundation to drive your activities.

Based on research and market information, the key pillars of employee experience are as per Figure 2-1.

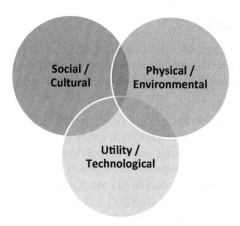

Figure 2-1. Employee experience pillars

- **The Social/Cultural Pillar**: This pillar is all about the interactions and relationships employees create, develop, and sustain with one another that can impact the individual and the team effectiveness and perceptions within the organization.

- **The Physical/Environmental Pillar**: This pillar is about the configuration, design, and interactions of employees with their workspaces. This includes furniture, equipment, and communal spaces. This pillar as well is about the environmental factors such as lighting, temperature, and wellness offers provided to increase the mental and physical interactions with the environment and keep the stimulation to the highest effective level.

- **The Utility/Technological Pillar**: This pillar is all about the digital capabilities, adoption, and frictionless experience of employees with their tools, technology, and software solutions. I believe that this pillar will have the biggest impact in the future, knowing that the future is more virtual, more remote, and more inclusive. This pillar can make or break the employee experience of an organization.

In this book, I will provide you the details on how to tackle the last pillar through employee-centric IT. I will give you tools and concepts that will help you provide the employees the ultimate experience in how to trust you, engage with you, and frictionlessly use your tools along their journey.

Let's define what trust is in the next section.

Trust Equation

In the early 2000s, a total of 118 students from the University of Groningen in the Netherlands participated in a study to rate individuals along a number of different dimensions. None of the students in the study enrolled in psychology classes.

In every session that took about one hour, around 20–30 participants rated video tapes of 25 opposite-sex individuals. Every participant received €7.50 for their participation. After all ratings were completed, participants were randomly split into two experimental groups. The first group, identified as the hypothetical decision group, were asked to decide across a number of different situations how they would invest the €7.50 they had just earned. The participants in this group were informed that their decisions were strictly hypothetical and would have no real consequences to them. Nonetheless, they were explicitly encouraged to make the best decision as if this was a real situation.

In the second group, identified as the actual decision group, the participants were asked to make the same decisions; however, the situation is real, with real money.

In both groups, participants were informed that they were to make their decisions under full anonymity to others and to the experimenters.

The decisions that participants in both groups were asked to make were for the following two circumstances:

- **Decision 1**: If one participant (let's call them Person A) decided to give the money they just got to another participant (let's call them Person B), then Person B would receive €30 from the experimenter and had to choose between having an equal split of the €30, giving €15 back to Person A, and keeping all the money and returning nothing.

  - Participants were asked to indicate their own decisions as both Person A and Person B and estimated the percentage of their fellow participants who would give money back as Person B.

- **Decision 2**: Participants were asked if they keep €7.50 for sure or that they could buy a ticket for a lottery with that money. In case their ticket won, they would receive €15; in case their ticket lost, they would receive nothing.

  - Participants were informed that winning or losing would be decided by blind draw of a ball out of a basket with 100 balls, and participants indicated the minimum number of winning balls they would require before to induce them to buy a lottery ticket.

A similar study was conducted in the United States to check if the cultural dimension has any impact on results.

Both studies were conducted by Detlef Fetchenhauer, from the University of Cologne, and David Dunning, from Cornell University, with the goal to identify if people trust too much or too little. The results were astonishing.

Across two studies, participants trusted their peers too little, in that they didn't trust many of their peers would return money, prompting them to sacrifice profitable decisions to trust. However, participants also trusted too much. Given their high levels of cynicism and tolerance for risk, a few should have handed money over, yet many still chose to trust.

The preceding study highlights that trust is not purely rational nor can be driven by empirical data or drive. Trust needs effort and hard work to achieve and can be in no time broken. There are many models describing trust and the level of trustworthiness. As we are all humans, I like to translate achieving trust by winning the following two vital things, as illustrated in Figure 2-2:

- **Winning the Hearts**: You need to understand and listen to the employees' feelings and make them feel that you care. By winning their hearts, the employees will be open to challenges and mistakes and be more accepting when things take longer.

- **Winning the Minds**: You need to show and make the employees sense that your activities, actions, and transformations have real rigor and logic. By winning their minds, the employees are willing to support you, engage with you, and even contribute to the benefit of you and them.

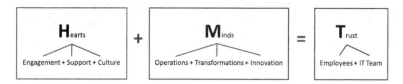

Figure 2-2. Trust equation

Employee-centric IT can only work if the employee trusts in IT. You will win the employees' trust by winning their hearts and minds. Then it allows you to engage and build a community of ambassadors that positively drive the organization through digital transformations with you and multiply the power of innovation, improvements, and speed of implementing new IT and technology and reaping the benefit for the entire organization.

The Checklist Is Born

In 1935, the United States Army Air Corps wanted to build its next-generation long-range bomber and asked three companies to bid for the contract. The Douglas Aircraft Co. was bidding with their Douglas DB-1, the Glenn L. Martin Co. with their Martin 146, and Boeing with their Model 299.

On paper, Boeing's Model 299 was superior in all aspects: it flew farther and faster, it carried more payload, and it was more advanced and sophisticated than the other two contenders. The last formality was an official flying demonstration before the Army was planning to order at least 65 of Boeing's aircraft.

On the day of demonstration, Model 299 lifted off and reached 300 feet but then stalled and crashed, killing two out of the five crew members, including the pilot. The investigation of the crash determined that pilot error caused the crash, forgetting to release a new locking mechanism while managing many controls. The analysis caused the Model 299 to be framed as "too complex to fly," and Boeing lost the contract.

Impacted with such a loss, a group of Boeing engineers and test pilots worked together to understand the source of the issue and brainstormed on possible solutions. There, a simple approach was agreed on: creating a pilot's checklist that covers key critical actions for the plane taxi, takeoff, and landing.

Their conclusion came after they jointly agreed that the airplane wasn't too complex to fly, but too complicated with a lot of sequential steps to be simply memorized by the pilot. Using a technicality in the bidding and selection process of the Army Air Corps, Boeing was able to ask for another demonstration with 12 Model 299 aircrafts and went to fly for 1.8 million miles without an accident. Ultimately, Boeing was able to provide more than 13,000 Model 299 to the Army, and it is believed that the Model 299, designated the B-17, gave the Allies an air advantage to win World War II.

This simple innovation, the checklist, is now a mandatory tool in routine and emergency conditions, in almost every industry we are in.

Summary

Extraordinary employee experience can only be achieved with employee-centric IT in your organization. IT teams can achieve employee-centricity by gaining the trust of their organization's employees. To achieve trust, IT organizations need to win the minds and hearts of every employee. In the next chapter, I will share the concepts that build up trust and will provide you checklists that will help you in executing those concepts.

Winning Employees' Hearts

On a very important day, Doug Dietz visited the hospital, proud and happy to see his newest machines installed. Doug worked on GE Healthcare's magnetic resonance imaging (MRI) equipment for many years, and his product is now complete and ready to be used. On his way out of the room, Doug saw a little girl, crying, terrified, and holding her parents' hands and didn't want to go inside the MRI room to take her scan. Doug heard the father leaning down and saying, "remember we talked about this; you can be brave."

After talking to the staff, Doug was shocked to hear that more than 80% of young patients had to be sedated to get them to lie still during the scan. Doug has beautifully designed great technology that works seamlessly for what it was created; however, at the beginning he missed the big picture – the user of the technology. Doug reflected on this and realized: "Everything was kind of like, beige, the room itself is dark and has those flickering fluorescent lights. The machine I had designed looked like a brick with a hole in it."

Doug took the challenge to improve the patient experience and later returned with an improved MRI experience for pediatric patients, reducing sedation to 10%; patient satisfaction at Children's Hospital of Pittsburgh, the first pilot, has gone up by 92%. You can get the details by watching his TED Talk: "The Design Thinking Journey: Using Empathy to turn Tragedy into Triumph."

Doug's story highlights the significance of how people feel toward technology will impact their engagement and adoption. Empathy is the primary aspect of winning the trust of people. People are driven by how they feel about something, whether physical, virtual, or both.

Research has shown that successful startups are only possible if there is full empathy between the team. Design thinking drives the new way of experiencing challenges through empathy and feelings.

In enterprise IT, this is a bigger challenge than in the consumer world because, in the consumer market, people choose the technology they feel most comfortable with, while in organizations, and at this moment in time, it is forced upon them.

Therefore, corporate IT must work smarter and harder to win employees' feelings. Employees must feel that IT listens to them, cares for them, and are willing to take the extra mile for them.

To be a truly employee-centric IT department, you will need to create intimacy with your employees personally, on a department and community level. You must exceed their expectations on the support and care you provide in digital and physical environments. And you will need to surpass their anticipations about aligning to their global and local corporate and country cultures.

In the *Power of Moments* book, both writers Chip and Dan Heath highlight that human beings are driven by moments and remember moments more than the entire experience. They show that humans remember the peaks and troths of experiences, and as long as the peaks are stronger than the other experiences, they can create those lasting moments. This is based on the Peak-End Rule, proposed by Barbara Fredrickson and Daniel Kahneman (Figure P2-1).

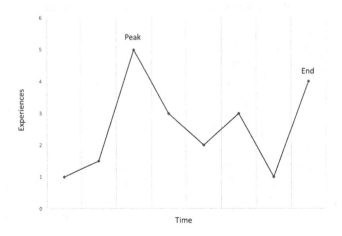

Figure P2-1. Fredrickson and Kahneman's "Peak-End Rule"

Within an enterprise, IT should find the balance between the needs of the employees and their wants and create those moments of connections to make their IT experience employee-centric, positive, epic, and expected.

So, let's dive deeper into how you can create engagement, exceed support, and build a culture that fosters a happy and satisfied employee with their IT and digital tools.

Winning the Engagement

Dominic Cobb is a skilled thief, the absolute best in the dangerous art of extraction and stealing valuable secrets. However, Dominic is not any kind of thief. Instead of breaking into a person's home, office, or even computer, he steals from deep within a person's subconscious while they are dreaming. Dominic has done many dangerous things, and he is now an international fugitive costing him everything he cares about. Now Dom is being offered a chance at redemption by pulling a reverse job: planting an idea rather than stealing one. The target is Robert Michael Fischer, the heir to an energy business empire. The process is called "inception." Why? Dominic said: What is the most resilient parasite? Bacteria? A virus? An intestinal worm? An idea. Resilient and highly contagious. Once an idea has taken hold of the brain, it's almost impossible to eradicate. An idea that is fully formed – fully understood – that sticks, right in there somewhere.

The preceding story is the plot of the 2010 movie *Inception* directed by Christopher Nolan and stars Leonardo DiCaprio as Dominic Cobb.

I mentioned the story to show how powerful the acknowledgment and feeling of acceptance of an idea could be if delivered in the right way at the right time. And this is the key ingredient for IT to win the engagement movement.

© Mark Ghibril 2023
M. Ghibril, *Employee-Centric IT*, https://doi.org/10.1007/978-1-4842-9186-3_3

In this digital world, the advantages are enormous compared to the purely physical world in the past.

Employees currently live longer hours in their virtual world than in their physical one. They interact more; they reach for help, advice, support, and engagement virtually more than they ever did in their physical life.

Research shows that you must be responsive and transparently open to create engagement and intimacy with others.

Responsiveness has two areas to tackle. The receptive area is where you need to be responsive to reactions/engagements initiated by the employees. The preemptive area is where you proactively act and respond to your employees based on your understanding of what they might require or expect.

Openness is to be fully transparent and honest about what you can deliver, what you know and don't know, and what you will be doing with the information you receive from your employees.

So how can you build this intimacy and engagement in the enterprise for your IT/digital engagements? With many failures, learnings, and improvements, I suggest building your engagement on two layers – employee and community (Figure 3-1).

Figure 3-1. Employee and community layers

Employee Engagement

As humans, empathy, intimacy, and engagement are built on personal relationships. The most common negative feedback in IT satisfaction surveys is that IT has no face or lack of real human to be able to talk to, listen to the employees, and take their issues forward. To tackle it is to bring the human close to your employees by having IT employees dedicated to employee engagement. These employees should have their roles defined in a way that purely concentrates on engagement, intimacy, and employee satisfaction. Their skills and experience should be concentrated on listening, care, and problem-solving rather than your typical technical skills. Technical skills are a plus, of course, but are not mandatory. Experience showed me that strong interpersonal and communications skills would be better than having the needed technical skills. The key skills you should look at are as follows:

- Understanding of how people go through a change and the change process

- Listening and communication skills

- Flexibility and adaptability to different situations

These employee engagement team members are acting as the face of IT toward the employees, the bridge between employees and the real technical teams. They will act on both reactive and proactive responsiveness:

- Reactive in responding to unhappy employees due to certain engagements with IT on support channels

- Reactive in responding to feedback and comments by employees on any company channels (e.g., email, social network, intranet)

- Proactive in communicating about transformations and change activities and projects

- Proactive in providing training and information on digital and productivity tools

- Proactive in measuring the pulse of the employees and proactively driving improvements in employee experience and satisfaction

- Proactive in offering advice to maximize the use of technology

As for the setup, employee engagement team members shouldn't replace your IT support channels or personnel, but they should be the face of IT concerning engagement. This presence doesn't have to be physical as well. Irrespective of the medium, these team members should be accessible to your employees, and how to reach them needs to be clear, simple, and easy.

Usually, businesses or even some IT departments react in the short term and request IT presence purely to be fully driven by business, concentrated on technical skills, and sort out shortsighted problems. If you react to such demands, it will be like a drug addiction, where you can provide satisfaction for a short period but bad for the long term.

Community Engagement

In the book *Tribes* and his TED Talk about it, Seth Godin says that the idea of "tribes," which dates back 50,000 years, is about people who always wanted to be in a group connected in special-purpose ideas and building a community.

Equivalently in a professional environment, a community (or what is called now a community of practice) is a group of employees, either in one department or now more and more cross-departmental communities have a common interest, common use of tools, and the common need for digital and IT knowledge. I suggest you build the competence center of employee engagement to tackle those. This group of people acts as the franchise for your entire IT/digital department. They build the brand, the experience, and communications to be consistent, employee-centric, and clear. They also take and build engagement with communities to enhance responsiveness and openness with the entire organization.

These communities can be around business topics, business departments, processes, and projects/programs or need to be built by the IT team around tools and transformation and change activities.

There is only so much information that we can keep in our heads as humans. Therefore, a community is a way to store and share knowledge in the collective and quickly get help, tips and tricks, and new ideas to improve productivity and use of digital tools for the benefit of the business.

The power of the community allows you to achieve two things:

- Create a space where your IT teams can engage with the community on one to N scale.

- Build the knowledge of the community to a level it becomes self-sufficient to drive its digital knowledge and engagement. This reduces the effort in orchestrating the community and allows you to concentrate on driving the topics.

With this, communities will also identify and supercharge your "super" users who will become your change agents, ambassadors, and frontline multipliers within their departments, locations, and businesses.

Self-Assessment

To initiate where you are on this journey, I suggest you assess the following key capabilities you have today:

– Do you have IT team members or even business team members who are working as the human listening machine for employees regarding their IT tools, issues, and understanding?

– Do you have an employee engagement competence center in place encompassing all your IT members that engage with your employees worldwide?

– Do you have communities set up across processes and digital/IT tools and that are cross-departmental?

If you have all three of the preceding key capabilities, then you are winning the engagement. If not, then you can follow the following checklist to help you move forward.

Checklist

Preparation Steps

– Identify your employee engagement capabilities:

- Analyze the skills of team members who are performing your "last mile" IT activities, which include onsite support, business-facing team members, project managers, and change managers.

- Document their responsibilities, resources, and distribution across the countries/locations.

– Identify your community engagement capabilities:

- Analyze the communities you have in place and the topics they cover.

- Do any of your communities have moderators, knowledge experts, and cross-functional employees?

Problem-Solving Steps

– Create an employee engagement competence center, covering the responsibilities around

- Developing employee interaction, readiness, and adoption methods and concepts to enhance engagement

- Managing IT/digital training, roadshows, and events to be used across your organization

- Developing user and customer satisfaction concepts to measure, analyze, and improve employee satisfaction with IT

- Developing communities of practice concepts

- Ensure coverage of employee engagement team members across all your operations to complement your employee engagement competence center to ensure local:

  - Training and support to relevant communities

  - Ensuring employee proximity and care by implementing engagement initiatives

  - Coaching employees to make full use of their IT/digital tools

Prevention Steps

- To avoid pushback and defensive response from your IT teams, assign a change management team to work closely with your IT leaders. This team should assist the IT leaders to understand the benefit such employee and community engagement team members will bring. Without such change management activities, you will struggle to get traction.

Summary

Winning the engagement should create the following:

- The feeling of intimacy and engagement, irrespective of the channel and time.

- The feeling of responsiveness and openness for winning the hearts of the employees.

- Engage with the individual and the community and ensure distance doesn't matter.

Winning the Support

Skyla, an accountant, started one day experiencing the most excruciating pain in her upper abdomen. The pain episodes at first lasted about four minutes. Even though she knew she should go to the hospital, she felt better and decided not to go as soon as the pain went away. After experiencing the pain for a longer period (longer than normal), she made an appointment with the doctor.

She arrived at the doctor's office one morning. During that morning, she didn't have any pain. When she entered the analysis room, she was asked many questions. They took blood and urine tests and sent her back home and told her they would call with the results. When she got the call, the tests were good, and the doctor confirmed to her that there was nothing to worry about and that it would go away.

However, Skyla inside felt and knew something had to be wrong. About a week later, she was woken up by the pain, and this time it lasted more than 30 minutes and didn't go away. She couldn't even get out of bed due to the pain. So she quickly called the ambulance. The pain diminished by the time the ambulance got to her (around 20 minutes later). The paramedics assumed that she was faking because the pain was less, and she could walk. The fact that they didn't believe her made her more agitated.

© Mark Ghibril 2023

M. Ghibril, *Employee-Centric IT*, https://doi.org/10.1007/978-1-4842-9186-3_4

She was taken to the hospital as she insisted, and she was checked again and this time diagnosed with appendicitis and had to undergo emergency surgery. The surgery went OK; however, she had some minor complications, which caused her a hematoma (localized bleeding outside of blood vessels due to the surgery).

A month later, Skyla was with her boyfriend on their way to celebrate their third anniversary when the pain returned. She asked her boyfriend to take her to a different hospital and doctor. The current hospital and doctor did not listen to her and her symptoms and did not take her seriously. The different hospital and doctors were much more attentive, listened to her, did the same blood and urine tests (as the first doctor/hospital), and finally correctly diagnosed her with pancreatitis caused by a gallbladder stone. Skyla had these "attacks," as she likes to call them, eight times before she was finally taken seriously enough to "fix" her. Since they removed her gallbladder, Skyla had no pain.

Skyla is a fictitious name; however, the preceding story is true and happened to a real lady.

The preceding story is common in the medical industry, and according to studies

- Only 36% of patients are given the opportunity to speak comfortably about their symptoms and reason for going to a doctor/hospital.

- 92 seconds is the longest average time given to a patient to talk about their symptoms before they are interrupted (30 seconds for primary care doctor).

- Even worse, only 20% of specialty care doctors even asked their patients what was wrong.

36% of patients are given the opportunity to speak comfortably about their symptoms and reason for going to a doctor/hospital	92 seconds is the longest average time given to a patient to talk about their symptoms before they are interrupted	20 percent of specialty care doctors even asked their patients what was wrong

Figure 4-1. Data from the medical industry

A study in Canada highlighted key areas:

- An initial patient interview is crucial for "focused, efficient, and patient-centered care."
- Listening to patients is an essential component of clinical data gathering and diagnosis.
- Listening is as healing and therapeutic as the session itself.
- Listening fosters and strengthens the doctor-patient relationship.

So why am I mentioning this? IT support is the IT care ecosystem for employees, and the IT agents are the digital doctors for employees. And as the preceding example, most companies have an IT support setup in place; however, they miss two crucial areas:

- Focused and employee-centered "care"
- Listening

In addition, most IT satisfaction survey results and benchmarks have consistently rated the IT service desk at the lowest scales of such surveys.

This is a dichotomy as IT support is the face of IT and digital while it is the worst perceived service.

The good news is that with the right digital support ecosystem, you can build an employee-centric organization that the employees can trust and want to engage with. In addition, they can become your brand ambassadors with their fellow employees.

So what are we looking for in IT support? We should first understand the challenges/problems employees have and their expectations of those challenges to define what IT support should offer.

There are three kinds of problems: simple (like baking a cake from a mix – few repeatable techniques), complicated (like building a car – multiple people and coordination but repeatable), and complex (like raising a child, always a different approach required).

Figure 4-2. Problem complexity distribution

1 – Simple Problems

Simple problems are usually the highest percentage of problems (approx. 80% of IT support problems on average). However, the expectations for resolution are quite high. Most employees still use a search engine like Google or Bing when they don't know how to do something in their personal and professional lives. But when things break at work, employees expect to get quick, easy access to how-to content from your organization across various channels.

2 – Complicated Problems

Complicated problems are usually around 15% of problems and require more than simple, easy access to how-to content. The employees want to have easy access to the right experts to diagnose and coordinate the resolution for their problems.

3 – Complex Problems

These are usually 5% of the problems and require multiple teams to work together to resolve the issue. Instead of speaking to a faceless person, employees would like to feel like talking to someone with the same experiences and understanding.

So why should you differentiate your problems? First, a study by McKinsey revealed that there is a vast difference in efficiency between personal service, self-service, and crowd service. If the cost of personal service is 100%, then self-service amounts to 12% and crowd service to 9%, so there's a huge discrepancy. Gartner, the research company, estimates that using communities to solve support issues reduces costs by 50% and enhances user satisfaction, as long as you know what you can cover in your communities, from expertise and product.

Therefore, to achieve successful employee-centered IT support, we need to provide communities and IT support agents that take end-to-end ownership and care of the employee's issues, complaints, and problems. They need to offer them "focused and employee-centered care." In addition, we need them to listen attentively and authentically to understand the problem and help, rather than follow certain KPIs. Here, listening is the ultimate skill that every person involved in IT support should possess.

Let's jump into how to achieve focused and employee-centered care and listening culture within your IT organization.

Focused and Employee-Centered "Care"

At Princeton University, researchers John M. Darley and C. Daniel Batson recruited students to study how situational variables influence helping behavior.

The students were put in two groups and were asked to fill out a personality questionnaire. Both groups were asked to begin the procedures in one building and then go to another building to continue with a presentation. The key test was not about the personality but about the amount of urgency they have altered between the two groups. The researchers told the first group that they were late for the next task in the next building, while they told the second group that they had time but should head on over anyway.

On the way to the other building, the researchers put a man, slumped and hurt, in an alleyway. The students didn't know about that man or his condition. The researchers wanted to test the variables that influence the helping behavior of the group toward that man. On arrival at the second building, both groups were asked to fill out a questionnaire on helping behavior.

The researchers found that "hurriness" or "urgency" provided to the group significantly affected the helping behavior. In the same study, researchers identified that the topic of the presentation didn't have any influence on the helping behavior – that is, helping behavior wasn't influenced by the type of students or their studies.

This research confirms that to offer real and consistent "care," your IT support team has to be well trained to offer help, care, and support to the same level of quality, even in times of difficulty or crisis.

You can achieve this level of care through the following:

- **Empowering Your Agents**: Empowering your agents and IT support staff to own the employees' issues and have the right understanding of your IT organization to resolve the topics quickly

    - In all the organizations I worked in, IT agents hand over the tickets to the next levels of experts if they cannot resolve it and lose the oversight. Agents are not measured on the end-to-end ticket resolution but simply on the ones they could resolve themselves.

- **Turn This Around**: Each IT agent owns all the tickets in their queues and is empowered to force and chase other levels in the organization to resolve the ticket to the employee's expectations.

- To achieve it, you require a change in the mentality of your IT agents (might even need to change the level of expertise there), in your expert levels, and the entire operations teams.

- **Making Your Agents Human-Centered**

  - Train your agents on situations of "hurriness" or "urgency" and ensure they can consistently be listening to and valuing the employees' issues/requests, building a personal level of interaction with them, and offering them a "one"-stop shop for their issues.

  - Your agents also have to show their faces, make themselves known to the employees, and be accessible. Your employees will feel that they are talking to an individual rather than a simple "queue" owner who will not remember the employee the next time they open a ticket or chase on their current one.

Listening

In a study by cognitive psychologist Polly Dalton, 45 people aged between 16 and 47 were asked to listen to a recording through headphones. The recording simulated a party with two women and two men, where the women were wrapping up a present while the two men were preparing food and drinks. Half of the participants were asked to listen to the women's conversation, and half were asked to attend to the men's conversation. After listening to the scene, all participants were asked two questions:

- Did you hear anything unusual that didn't fit in with the scene?

- Did you hear anyone other than the four people preparing for the party?

The results were fascinating. While 90% of participants who were asked to listen to the men's conversation have mentioned that they heard the "I'm a gorilla" phrase, 70% of participants who were asked to listen to the women's conversation hadn't notice or heard the phrase. This phenomenon is coined as the "inattentional deafness" – "the absence of attention causes people to miss sounds that are otherwise easily detectable," says Polly. She also said:

"most of our participants found it hard to believe that they had missed such an unusual and distinctive sound, particularly given that it lasted for 19 seconds."

This experiment demonstrates how listening can vary and can be less effective if the participant is given a direction on what to listen to rather than attentively listening to the other person.

Inattentional deafness is what is happening exactly in the IT support world. The agents are provided with many checklists to follow and exact questions to ask, but they are not trained to listen. It has been getting worse over the past few decades. The issues in IT are moving from simple to more complex and cover a multitude of applications. In addition, the complexity of the IT landscape, from hardware proliferation (e.g., employees have laptops, phones, tablets, and some VR headsets) and application upsurge, makes consistent IT support across all these applications and hardware fairly complex.

The IT agents and support have to master the art of listening, which is a complex but vital feature if you want to achieve employee-centric IT support. IT agents have to

- Provide authenticity in the way they listen to understand the deep root of the issue

- Ask the right questions to provide the feeling that they are attentively listening to their challenges

- Respond in a caring manner showing their attitudes and intentions are fully for the employee's benefit

Every employee is different, and IT agents must listen to achieve the most comfortable communication channel.

With such listening, the employee interaction will be associated with a greater likelihood that all complaints or issues will be revealed early on and reduce the late issues.

Self-Assessment

To self-assess the status of your IT support ecosystem, I suggest you assess the following key capabilities you have today:

- Do you empower your IT agents to own the end-to-end accountability of the employee's incidents?

- Do you measure your IT agents' performance using end-to-end indicators regarding the employee's problem resolution?

- Do you hire and develop your IT agents on soft skills such as communication, listening, and conflict resolutions?

- Do you offer multiple types of support channels depending on the complexity of the employee's problems?

If you have all four of the preceding key capabilities, then you are winning the support. If not, then you can follow the subsequent checklist to help you move forward.

Checklist

Preparation Steps

- Analyze your IT support ecosystem from the perspective of

  - Channels offered to employees that they can contact IT for help in their problems. Analyze the official channels offered by the IT support ecosystem and the information channels that employees use to simply get their problem solved.

  - Analyze the accountability and ownership for all the different support levels you have (from IT agents to experts that are within your organization or your delivery partners). I suggest here again to check the formal contractual levels and their scope as well as the informal activities that are happening.

  - Analyze the percentage of problems you have that can be considered as simple, complicated, and complex.

- Analyze the soft skills of your IT operations team as a whole, especially the IT agents that engage with the employees to resolve their problems. Analyze their

  - Communication skills in standard situations and in complicated and stressful situations

  - Listening skills covering understanding and acknowledging/reconfirming

  - Conflict management under different situations, from time-sensitive to critical personally charged situations

- Analyze the performance indicators you are driving with your IT employees across the entire support ecosystem.

Problem-Solving Steps

- Develop a support channel strategy taking into consideration the problem complexities and communicate it.

    - The employees should be able to reach out to your teams from any of those channels, and your IT agents can then redirect the problem to the right channel as they see fit.

    - Ensure you have self-service, assisted, and fully personalized support and size them based on the type of problems and volume you have within your organization.

    - Here is my guidance on the use of channels based on their complexity:

        - For simple issues, self- or crowd service can be your best and cheapest support service. However, content quality and channel responsiveness are key to keeping your employees happy.

        - For complicated problems, you have to offer one-to-many communication between your employees and your experts and support group(s). It can be a community of practice with a higher degree of expertise and knowledge of certain IT products. Therefore, they can work with the employee in a social media tool context, a discussion forum, or a chat room with the support team. Or it can be a chat or phone interaction. In complicated problems, the employees' expectation is the feeling of care, and therefore ease of access, availability of channels and experts, and the response rate are key.

        - In complex issues, a personal service is the most efficient service, costly but the one that keeps your employees engaged and loyal to your service, brand, and product. Personal is face to face, such as drop-in centers or personal visits of the engineer, phone calls, or 1-2-1 chat. The self-service here is NOT recommended.

- Redefine the roles of your IT agents and provide them full ownership of any problem they get assigned.

  - Be sure to communicate this ownership and empowerment to the rest of your IT support teams.

  - Define and run an "employee-centric care" training program that all your IT agents and support teams should go through providing the key skills, processes, and activities that you expect from them to achieve employee-centric care. Rerun this training program every six months at the beginning and adapt it as you learn what is working and what needs improvement.

- Define your performance indicators for all your IT support teams to be the same, covering the end-to-end resolution of problems as well as employee satisfaction.

  - Having common performance indicators will drive the right mentality within your IT support teams, and your IT agents will then get the required attention and support from the expert teams when needed.

Prevention Steps

- To prevent your IT support teams and especially your IT agents from reverting back to the old way of working and accountability (not in my queue, not my problem mentality), deliver consistent communications and reiterations of the importance of the employee-centric care within your entire IT organization.

- Celebrate and share to your entire organization the "employee-centric care mavericks" and let your organization keep the pressure on your teams about the expectation you have set.

- Rotate your IT support teams between all levels of support so everyone gets the view of the "day in the life of" their colleagues in the support ecosystem and allow all to develop an empathy and understanding of their colleagues' challenges to support your mission to achieve best-in-class employee-centric care.

Summary

In summary, the ultimate IT support ecosystem should be focused and employee-centric. It is achieved through the right balance between assisted interactions, whether face to face, over the phone, or via chat, and unassisted digital interactions. In addition, employee-centric IT support teams that master listening can

- Identify early outcomes of matters of urgency
- Reduce stress on agents and employees
- Instill confidence in the direction of proposed solutions or next steps, which ensures employees will follow through on their side of the topic
- Foster a deeper connection between employees and agents
- Cultivate a new employee-centric IT relationship that can generate connections that will come up with new ideas, improvements, and satisfaction across the organization

Winning the Culture

In the mid-1950s, twenty-two 11-year-old boys were taken to a summer camp in Robbers Cave State Park, Oklahoma. These boys were not aware they were the subjects of an experiment. Before the trip, the boys were randomly divided into two groups.

The groups were housed in separate cabins and, for the first week, did not know about the existence of the other group. They were left to spend time bonding with each other. They could choose a name for their group and be stenciled on their shirts and flags. Group 1 was the Eagles and the other the Rattlers.

After the first week, the two groups were made aware of each other, and soon enough, signs of intergroup conflict emerged, mainly in verbal abuse.

The experimenters wanted to increase the conflict substantially. To do this, they set the groups against each other in competitions. The Rattlers won the overall trophy and could claim the ball field by planting their flag in it. Soon the groups refused to eat in the same room together.

With the conflict between the groups successfully instigated, the experiment moved into its final phase – trying to preach peace and acceptance between both groups. The experimenters tried different activities, such as watching a film and shooting firecrackers, but neither worked.

© Mark Ghibril 2023
M. Ghibril, *Employee-Centric IT*, https://doi.org/10.1007/978-1-4842-9186-3_5

The experimenters then tried a new approach. They took the two groups to a new location and gave them a series of problems to try and solve. In the first problem, the boys were told the drinking water supply had been attacked by vandals. The first seeds of peace were sown after the two groups successfully worked together to unblock a faucet. In the second problem, the two groups had to club together to pay for the movie they wanted to watch. Both groups also agreed on which movie they should watch. By the evening, the members of both groups were once again eating together.

The groups "accidentally" came across more problems over the next few days that needed them to work together to resolve them. Finally, the boys decided to travel home together on the same bus. Peace had broken out all over.

This experiment was done by Muzafer Sherif, who proved his realistic conflict theory (also called realistic group conflict theory), the idea that group conflict can result from competition over resources. Sherif also reached an important conclusion from this experiment and other research that groups naturally develop their own cultures, status structures, and boundaries, and this can cause internal and external conflicts. Sherif's key outcome is that a superordinate culture that stretches beyond the group itself must exist for groups to work together effectively and reduce conflict.

So what is culture and specifically "digital culture"? Based on a few definitions I have seen, I think the best and simplest definition of culture is as follows:

"the total sum of the beliefs, rules, techniques, practices, and artifacts characterize a group and allow them to communicate, collaborate and shape their environment and future."

Of course, the complexity of the global world that you regularly have cross-cultural experiences and interactions might test or challenge the cultural elements you are used to within your personal or professional lives. In addition, with the new digital world, another dimension comes in: the merge of the physical and virtual interactions, including digital tools and processes, which also brings different experiences and expectations based on your current cultural values.

With this in mind, I believe the definition of "digital culture" can be as follows:

"The total sum of interactions, principles, tools, and mediums that a group agrees to and allow them to communicate effectively, collaborate efficiently, and utilize the right technology to succeed in the digital world."

With this definition, you understand why building the right digital culture from an IT perspective will harness a better engagement with your employees across the entire organization. This digital culture has to cover the areas of communications, collaboration, and technology.

Figure 5-1. Digital culture elements

Ignoring cultural differences represents the largest stumbling block for global enterprises and IT teams. There is a word even that causes this stumbling block: ethnocentrism, which is evaluating other cultures from one's own cultural view and the belief that one's way of doing things is superior to that of others.

The challenge lies in recognizing differences, combining the advantages, adjusting, and adapting to succeed with different people, in different partnerships, and different physical and digital virtual mediums.

Let's jump into the key areas of communications, collaboration, and technology to support.

Communication

650 English-speaking adults from the United States were surveyed to understand better how people perceive the subtle difference between statements even if they do not realize it.

The researchers divided study participants into five conditions, each with 128 people.

Participants read variations of a paragraph that summarized research that showed a lack of gender differences in math skills. The text for each condition was identical except for a subtle difference in how the main finding was framed. Participants read text with one of four statements: "girls do just as well as boys at math," "boys do just as well as girls at math," "girls and boys are equally good at math," and "boys and girls are equally good at math."

After reading the text, all participants were asked which gender they considered more naturally skilled at math.

Of those participants who read a text that included "girls are as good as boys at math," 71% said boys have more natural math ability. But only 32% of participants said the same after reading a text that contained "boys are as good as girls at math," according to the research.

When the researchers explicitly asked participants if they thought the sentence "girls are as good as boys at math" was biased, people rated the statement as unbiased. This shows that the power of such statements to imply inequality occurs without listeners realizing it, the researchers said.

This research highlights that communications and language are intertwined. When people talk about cross-cultural communication, the question asked most frequently is, "How can we ensure mutual language fluency among speakers from different cultures?".

Therefore, IT teams must ensure their communications and language are very effectively studied to ensure it reaches the right impact and understanding.

Communication style needs to capture both directive and advice-oriented elements to reach cultures at both ends of the spectrum.

Communications should provide both individualistic and collectivist reasoning of the benefits of your request. Leaving one or the other reason will alienate the relevant culture. In addition, visual and verbal communications are key.

Context is your silver bullet in all dimensions. Your communication has to have a clear context that provides a clear direction but leaves space for all cultures to take what fits their cultures. It is easier said than done, but you automatically see the difference in engagement when done right.

Informal conversations and communication are also key to building trust and relationship between all team members. And there is nothing as "overcommunicate." Your communication needs to ensure you touch both the hearts and the minds of people. Always mix the visual/physical communication to allow different cultures to process the information and minimize uncertainty. The key here is to develop cohorts beyond your core team to help with consistent communication and feedback. Direct and full-bodied communication is always required and with the right blend of data and facts.

Finally, acknowledging both opportunities and constraints for a certain situation should be included in your messages to avoid anyone dismissing your communication.

Collaboration

In 1993, Ray Dalio, the chairman of the Bridgewater Associates, the largest hedge fund globally, received a memo signed by his top three executives who were surprisingly honest in assessing him.

This memo was an upward feedback on his performance, mentioning both the positive and the negative attributes. "Ray sometimes says or does things to employees which makes them feel incompetent, unnecessary, humiliated, overwhelmed, belittled, pressed or otherwise bad," the memo read. "If he doesn't manage people well, growth will be stunted, and we will all be affected."

This memo was both devastating and a wake-up call to Ray.

This moment pushed Ray to drive a change in the culture inside his company, one based on principles that place "radical transparency" above everything else. He drove a sense of humility, transparency and radical honesty, and openness within his company.

Ray's principles have been released in a book, *Principles: Life and Work*, which provides a detailed overview of all principles he and everyone in Bridgewater follow.

This example of transparency emphasizes the importance of the collaboration level between IT and the rest of the organization.

To reach radical transparency and collaboration within your employee-centric organization, collaboration must be tackled openly, be radically transparent, and create a culture of openness and essential collaboration.

All your IT team members have to be radically collaborative with each other and the rest of the organization. This means

- Collaboration has the right mix of personal and teamwork.

- Utilize motivation and gamification to allow your IT team members and employees to feel they can work together for their satisfaction. Don't forget to celebrate achievements, physically and virtually.

- Use Agile and design thinking frameworks to reduce conflict due to hierarchy.

- Use multiple media-rich channels as well as face-to-face interactions.

- Collaboration requires debate, and therefore time should be given to discuss, challenge, and come up with ideas.

Technology

The right technology will ensure your right culture is accessible across the entire organization:

- Ensure you have technologies that flatten the hierarchy. Such tools could be enterprise social networks (such as Yammer, Socialcast, Slack) or social intranets (such as Jive, Unily), where power is eliminated through information democratization.

- With the wide spectrum of cultures and allowing all their inclusion, I suggest allowing content anonymity to allow people to freely contribute ideas and feedback without feeling that they are impacting the interest of their group. In addition, the adoption of technology will vary between individualistic and collectivist cultures and change management for such rollouts has to be different based on the culture.

- Gamification technology and tools are a must. Using online tools that cover both emotional and behavioral concepts of gamification is key (more on this in the next chapter). Technology has a big role in offering media-rich, multichannel options for people to collaborate and communicate in an immersive way, catching the minds and emotions of the team members.

- Video conferencing rooms and desktop options are a must, and integrated interactive rooms and boards will help. Analytical tools that allow easy access to data visualization could help you keep the factual data at your fingertips while setting the scene of the activity. In addition, virtual and physical boards and post-it notes for brainstorming and check-ins are vital. Group instant messaging and social tools are a must to allow and provide the platform for discussions, collaboration, and alignment.

Self-Assessment

To self-assess your IT culture, please check these key capabilities:

- Does your communication have the entire spectrum of context, reasoning, and style to reach and be consumed correctly by your entire organization?

- Do you encourage and have a radically transparent collaboration between IT and the rest of the organization?

- Have you implemented the right mix of technologies to allow you to communicate effectively and collaborate transparently across the organization?

If you have all three of the preceding key capabilities, then you are winning the culture. If not, then you can follow the subsequent checklist to help you drive toward the right ultimate goal of winning the culture.

Checklist

Preparation Steps

- Evaluate your IT communication by

  - Reviewing your communications context, style, and reasoning currently utilized across all your IT communications

  - Identifying if an organization-wide communication style handbook exists that you can tap on to drive a common type of communications toward your employees

  - Capturing feedback from a sample of your employees around your communications context, style, and reasoning effectiveness as well as the channels these communications have been delivered on

- Evaluate your IT collaboration by

  - Assessing the collaboration efficiency between your IT teams and the rest of the organization through

  - Simple analysis of the amount of collaboration meetings that are IT internal only vs. with the rest of the organization

  - Identifying the collaboration challenges

Problem-Solving Steps

- Develop a support channel strategy taking into consideration the problem complexities and communicate it.

  - The employees should be able to reach out to your teams from any of those channels, and your IT agents can then redirect the problem to the right channel as they see fit.

- Ensure you have self-service, assisted, and fully personalized support and size them based on the type of problems and volume you have within your organization.

- Redefine the roles of your IT agents and provide them full ownership of any problem they get assigned.

    - Be sure to communicate this ownership and empowerment to the rest of your IT support teams.

    - Define and run an "employee-centric care" training program that all your IT agents and support teams should go through providing the key skills, processes, and activities that you expect from them to achieve employee-centric care. Rerun this training program every six months at the beginning and adapt it as you learn what is working and what needs improvement.

- Define your performance indicators for all your IT support teams to be the same, covering the end-to-end resolution of problems as well as employee satisfaction.

    - Having common performance indicators will drive the right mentality within your IT support teams, and your IT agents will then get the required attention and support from the expert teams when needed.

Prevention Steps

- To prevent your IT support teams and especially your IT agents from reverting back to the old way of working and accountability (not in my queue, not my problem mentality), deliver consistent communications and reiterations of the importance of the employee-centric care within your entire IT organization.

- Celebrate and share to your entire organization the "employee-centric care mavericks" and let your organization keep the pressure on your teams about the expectation you have set.

- Rotate your IT support teams between all levels of support so everyone gets the view of the "day in the life of" their colleagues in the support ecosystem and allow all to develop an empathy and understanding of their colleagues' challenges to support your mission to achieve best-in-class employee-centric care.

Summary

Achieving the right culture in your IT organization is hard but rewarding. By mastering the three elements of culture – communications, collaboration, and technology – you will be able to achieve a culture that is inclusive, supportive, and employee-centric.

Communication relies on the context and has to be done on multiple layers to ensure it reaches all employees in your organization, irrespective of their backgrounds, personal cultures, and experiences.

Collaboration will only work if it is radically transparent, honest, and engaging in both the physical and digital channels.

Technology must be right, cohesive, and accessible to all employees to allow them to collaborate and communicate effectively, transparently, and reliably.

So now you have the right concepts and tools to win the hearts of your employees and are a step closer to become a best-in-class employee-centric IT team. As the saying goes, a heart without a head is halfway there only. Let's jump into what you can do to win their minds and transform them!

Winning Employees' Minds

In a study conducted by Gloria Mark of the University of California, 48 German university students were put in a simulated office environment and were given an email task to execute. They were asked to play a human resource manager of a medium-sized company and that they had just returned from holidays. They were carefully instructed to answer all their emails quickly, correctly, and politely. The participants were given a fact sheet that helped them answer the emails.

The participants were told that their supervisor (an experimenter sat in another room) would contact them periodically and ask questions.

There were three different groups:

- One group had no interruptions.

- Another group was interrupted with questions concerning the human resource context (e.g., "How many employees, including you, are in the department today?").

- The third group was interrupted with questions that differed from their known topics (e.g., "How many hot dogs do we need for 240 employees?").

These interruptions were designed to simulate the types of interruptions one might expect in an office environment. Participants were instructed to attend to interruptions immediately, such as picking up the telephone or responding to an instant message.

The results were fascinating: even though interruption didn't have a disruptive impact on productivity, as other research has highlighted, this research still showed that tasks were completed, even in less time, with no difference in quality. However, this came at a price for the participants: participants who got interrupted experienced more stress, higher frustration, time pressure, and effort.

I mention this study as 70% of employees depend on digital tools to do their daily work in today's world. In addition, 60% of employees are now "locationless": not working from one location, which means any interruption to these tools is causing them frustration, more stress, and overloaded feelings.

IT is now not only a support function but an enabling function. Without it, companies simply can't operate. And for employees to trust IT, they need to think that the IT and digital tools and landscape available for them are the right tools. They can use them effectively, are introduced to them efficiently, and are always provided with the latest technology to support their daily work.

A Deloitte research identified that generally employees are "overwhelmed" at work, and 72% of employees say they "cannot find the information they need within their company's information systems."

Therefore, to move into employee-centricity in everything you do in IT and get the employees to trust it, you should win their minds. This can be done by

- **Winning the Operations**: Ensure the day-to-day IT operations support employee stability (no interruptions), experience, and ease of use.

- **Winning the Transformation**: Any change or transformation activities you are running should be employee-centric driven and not technology driven.

- **Winning the Innovation**: Employees need to believe they are part of the innovative process and have a voice.

Figure P3-1. Winning employees' minds

We will dive deeper in each of the topics in the next three chapters and provide you insight, checklists, and actions you can do to win over your employees' minds. Chapter 6 will dive into IT operations, Chapter 7 into transformation, and we will finish this part with Chapter 8 and winning the innovation.

Winning the Operations

In the 1980s, a set of Stanford students were recruited for a study. The students were handed packets of information about a firefighter called Frank K.

Frank's bio mentioned he had a baby daughter and liked scuba diving. The packets also included Frank's responses to what the researchers called the Risky-Conservative Choice Test. According to one version, Frank was a successful firefighter who, on the test, almost always went with the safest option. Frank also chose the safest option in the other version, but he was a lousy firefighter who'd been put "on the report" by his supervisors several times.

Midway through the study, the students were informed that they'd been misinformed and that the information they'd received was entirely fictitious.

After that information, the students were asked to describe their beliefs about a successful firefighter's attitude toward risk. The students who'd received the first packet thought that successful firefighters would avoid it. The students in the second group thought a successful firefighter would embrace it.

Even after the evidence "for their beliefs has been refuted, people fail to make appropriate revisions in those beliefs," the researchers noted. "Once formed," the researchers observed dryly, "impressions are remarkably perseverant."

© Mark Ghibril 2023
M. Ghibril, *Employee-Centric IT*, https://doi.org/10.1007/978-1-4842-9186-3_6

The preceding study shows that changing employees' beliefs about IT will be tough if they are made up due to bad experiences, even if their beliefs have been refuted. Especially in operations, building employees' positive experiences can take time. Therefore, you should always spend enough energy to avoid the opinions and perceptions made as it will be way harder to change after.

In most organizations, IT operations teams (which usually concentrate on running thousands of applications and networks, ensuring they run effectively, securely, and seamlessly) spend very little time on employee experience. IT operations teams prefer to keep the lights on than concentrate on employee-centric issues. This way of work might have been possible to work in the past when IT operations dealt with purely the big applications and networks. However, this can no longer be sustained. Today, applications, networks, and security enable the employee to create outcomes, and we can't expect the employee to work around them.

So, employee-centric IT operations is a must, and to achieve it, this needs to be tackled on four fronts:

- **Data-Driven**: IT Operations data has to be available to all employees to educate them about what's happening.

- **Education-Driven**: Employees are now experiencing IT and not simply using it. Therefore, you need to provide them the best education to adopt and use the tools, every day.

- **Persona-Driven**: Employees are not alike in their IT consumption/use, and therefore you have to acknowledge it and make them aware of how their persona is being supported and operated by IT.

- **Productivity-Driven**: Continuous improvement on process and cost fronts is always a priority in operations. Improving the status quo activities should be employee-centric and ensure employees are informed about these activities, their contribution to the company bottom line, and involve them.

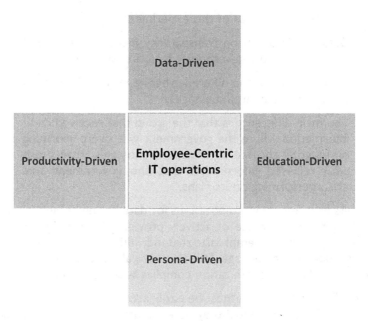

Figure 6-1. Four fronts of employee-centric IT operations

Let's tackle each of those four fronts in detail!

Data-Driven

In 2020, 1999 individuals living in the City of Buenos Aires, Argentina, were asked to participate in government activities. Participants were allocated at random to receive information about a series of commitments the government had made to the citizens of Buenos Aires. These commitments, made by the mayor when he took office, are tracked, and results are publicly available on the web page of the city government.

In addition, another random selection of participants was provided with two different articles, one highlighting the government pledge to efficiency and good management and another an empathetic message, where the government pledged to make life better for the inhabitants of the city.

Finally, all individuals received information showing either that the government was overperforming on its commitments or that the government was underperforming.

The participants were then asked to rate their trust in the government based on competence, honesty, and goodwill.

Three key outcomes came out of this experiment:

- Data and information transparency increased the trust/perception of the government by more than 10%.

- There was almost no difference between empathy-related and efficiency-related messages.

- The main difference is that the group that received data/information where the government was overperforming on its goals showed significantly higher trust than those who received information that the government was underperforming on its plans.

These results have important implications for data-driven organizations. First, they highlight the importance of actively providing information to enhance transparency. Second, they emphasize that individuals may not care that much about the framing of the message. Still, they care about the message's content, particularly whether the organization complies with its promises.

Therefore, IT operations data must be easily accessible by every employee in your company. They should feel they have full transparency on IT when they need it. Transparency of the health of your network, application performance, and even overall satisfaction will eliminate a lot of the "unwanted" noise from those who simply want to complain.

This can be done by providing access to online dashboards with all the data available. Of course, data alone can be interpreted in many ways. Your data must be provided so that both qualitative and quantitative information are available so any employee can read and understand the data in the same way.

This can be provided either through an AI solution, expanding on the graphs with textual information, or is updated regularly by your operational team.

Education-Driven

James Carse, the Director of Religious Studies at New York University, wrote a book, *Finite and Infinite Games*, exploring the difference between approaching life as a game with an end and a game that goes on forever. According to Carse, playing to win isn't nearly as satisfying as playing to keep the game going.

Carse argues that finite players spend their time in the past because that's where their winning is. Infinite players, in contrast, look to the future. Because their goal is to keep the game going, they focus less on what happened and put more effort into figuring out what's possible. By playing a single, nonrepeatable game, they are unconcerned with the maintenance and display of past status. They are more concerned with positioning themselves to deal effectively with whatever challenges.

According to Carse, "to be prepared against surprise is to be trained. To be prepared for surprise is to be educated." If you play a finite game, you train for the rules. Instead, if you play an infinite game, you focus on being educated to adapt to unknowns.

To win employees' minds and provide them with an extraordinary experience, you need to make your employees infinite players for IT. This will only be achieved by educating employees on IT tools, strategy, and information and not simply training them to use IT tools.

This can be achieved using gamification and game mechanics to engage your employees, solve problems, and provide users with incentives to behave in the desired way. Gamification uses mechanisms like points, badges, progress bars, and leaderboards to improve employee-centricity.

Based on my experience, I had few successes and failings with gamification. The best practice I have seen in the market is that applying gamification should be a planned, concrete, and considered campaign with a specific concept and mechanics that deal with a clearly defined business goal.

The three key pillars of such a gamification campaign are business goals, the gamification concept including mechanics and dynamics, and analytics.

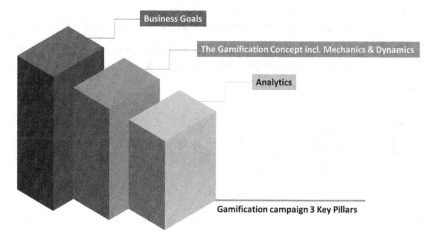

Figure 6-2. Gamification campaign three key pillars

The Business Goal

The key to any gamification implementation is understanding what you are trying to achieve, solve, or even capture. The business goal needs to be simple, specific, and measurable. For example, I see many companies implementing gamification to "improve employee satisfaction" as a business goal, and they are struggling to improve it. This is because employee satisfaction is a vast topic with various aspects and measurements. A better business goal can be to improve employee satisfaction by implementing gamification techniques to increase employee feedback on the customer relationship management tool. Another example is companies implementing gamification to "drive innovation" as a business goal. Another example of a specific and measurable business goal is "drive innovation by increasing the number of ideas submitted IT on improvements related to IT Operations dashboards".

The Gamification Concept Including Mechanics and Dynamics

The gamification concept needs to be "individualized" for each business goal. The concept should target your employee needs and the game mechanics and dynamics. Target areas you need to think of that will influence your concept are as follows:

A. **Behavioral vs. Emotional**: Do you want your employees to get involved in doing the particular activity physically or want their state of mind to be impacted positively by their engagement?

B. **Short Term vs. Long Term**: Do you want the business goal to be achieved in the short term or long term?

C. **Individual Level vs. Group Level**: Do you want the engagement on an individual, a group, or a collective level?

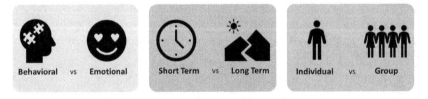

Figure 6-3. Target areas of the gamification concept

Based on your preceding answers, the following are my recommendations:

I. For behavioral-oriented concepts, the following types of gamification mechanics are most effective:

a. Points

b. Badges

c. Levels

II. For emotional-oriented concepts, the following types of gamification mechanics are most effective:

    a. Challenges/Quest

    b. Ratings

III. Based on the timeline of your goal, the use of rewards will need to be chosen:

    a. For short-term goals, use physical and virtual goods and achievement recognition.

    b. For long-term goals, use special/exclusive interactions and status recognition.

IV. Based on the level of engagement, use leaderboards for the individual level and progress bars for the group level.

Data Analytics

Of course, as the saying goes, "If you can't measure it, you can't manage it." Therefore, in any gamification implementation, the key is to ensure you capture the data at every possible interaction point (where possible).

Persona-Driven

At the National College of Art and Design (NCAD) in Dublin, a group of third year industrial design students were assigned a design project conducted over a period of five weeks. The students were divided into three groups, and the experimenters ensured equal strength of the students in each group. Two groups used personas as a design tool, and one group acted as the control group and did not use a persona-based approach. The objective of the experiment was to evaluate whether there was any difference in the final designs' usability. The study also sought to measure how using personas influenced the design teams' approaches to solving the brief.

The grades were awarded to the students at each stage. The overall grade was noted and revealed a clear pattern in completing the project. The teams that used personas scored higher than the control group, and the results indicate that the two groups with personas had a greater understanding of the user needs and designed solutions around the user-critical tasks to a greater degree than the control group.

The preceding results apply entirely to all IT activities, especially in operations. Personas strengthen the focus on the end user, their tasks, goals, and motivation. Personas make the end user's needs more explicit and can direct decision-making within operations teams more toward those needs.

There is no consensus on the number of personas in a corporation and the level of details needed to describe them. Even though I don't believe there is one size fits all, I think you have to consider the "operational" effort your team is willing to put into using the personas.

My experience has shown me that the more simple and concrete you have your personas defined, the more they will be utilized and more effective in meeting your goal.

Based on my research and experience, I suggest segmenting all your employees into four personas.

Digital Prophet   Digital Preacher   Digital Believer   Digital Atheist

4 Personas for all Employees

Figure 6-4. Four personas to segment your employees into

I – Digital Prophet

They are your employees who have the idea for your IT and digital products/ services, or they were the influence to make it exist. They believe they are superusers/experts on the tool, and their use of your IT tools makes or breaks it. They try to break the rules and use the tools they like rather than what you offer. However, they are the most connected and influential in their departments, and their colleagues will follow their lead.

2 – Digital Preacher

These are the early adopters, the mavericks, the champions for digital technology and products. They see digital products as replacements for unwanted physical activities and tasks and firmly believe in their value and benefit to their functions and company. If they believe in your IT products and services, they take it upon themselves to use them, promote them, and provide suggestions for improvement!

3 – Digital Believer

These are employees who believe in the IT products and tools they use. They are digital savvy and feel at ease in using IT, but some education and training might be required. However, they will only use the same or better-quality tools than older/nondigital products.

4 – Digital Atheist

These employees believe digital is only there for necessity and will only use it if no other nondigital product is available. They will resist and find excuses why they don't need, want, or can't use it.

I already hear some of you saying, what about demographics, geography, and other criteria? Have I missed those?

And I say, of course not! The preceding four personas are applicable irrespective of particular demography, geography, or culture.

The same person can be a different persona in their personal and corporate life. I know a lot of preachers in their personal lives that are either believers or even atheists in their corporate lives. Sometimes, it is caused by the status of the digital maturity in their corporate environment, and sometimes it is that they are two different personas between a private and corporate individual. You can and should add other criteria after you have identified your employees for a particular persona afterward to allow you to enhance your analysis and marketing engagement. For example, determining that all your digital believers have a specific age range or particular country/culture will help you personalize your communication activities and effectiveness.

Productivity-Driven

In 1979, four studies on adults and children were conducted to study the link between developmental increases in memory span and developmental increases in operational speed or efficiency. The memory span is the storage capacity of short-term memory or working memory. Span is the highest number of items that the subject can recall immediately, usually in the order in which the items were presented.

In the first experiment, the researchers asked 40 three- to six-year-old kids to repeat words in different spans. The second experiment tested ten adults on word repetition speed by manipulating word familiarity with six-year-olds from the first experiment. Their word spans were similar. The third experiment asked 84 five- to ten-year-olds to perform a counting span task. In the last experiment, 16 college students were tested on the speed of counting by forcing adults to count in an unfamiliar language; their counting spans were similar to six-year-olds previously tested.

The conclusion is that developmental increases in memory span do not result from increases in total processing space. Instead, with development, basic operations become faster and more efficient, meaning that they require less processing space and more space becomes available for storage.

The conclusion can be transmitted identically to IT operations. I mean that the critical development of IT operations is to make employees faster, more efficient, and cost-effective. With that, IT operations can then open up space in employees' minds for additional investment in transformational activities.

It is important to ensure your IT Operations activities become faster, more efficient, transparent, and felt by the employees. IT operations will deliver the backbone of the enterprise. Usually, it is not pretty from the outside, the view from employees, as people forget why you decided on certain activities that could impact their flexibility or experience. Therefore, IT operations have to be radically transparent on what is being done, provide the advantages provided to the enterprise as a whole, and, where needed, be very honest about the impact on the employees.

Employees will provide you with a "fresh start." They will understand your purpose, validate it, and support you day in and day out!

Self-Assessment

To self-assess your IT operations, please check these key capabilities:

- Does your IT operations team tackle the four fronts of employee-centricity?
  - Do you regularly provide transparent operational data that can be consumed by the employees at any time? Is this done manually or through an AI solution or integrated real-time dashboard?
  - Do you run educational gamification campaigns to enhance your employees' understanding of your IT Operations landscape?
    - Have you defined the business goals you want to achieve?
    - Have you assessed the target areas you want to influence?
    - Are you measuring consistently your outcomes?
  - Have you segmented your employees to different personas and tackled their knowledge, engagement, and experience accordingly?

- Are you very transparent and effective in communicating about the productivity measures you are driving and delivering for the overall organization to all your employees?

If you have all the preceding capabilities, then you are winning the operations, and you are one of the few performing all these tasks. If not or you need some help, let's jump to the checklist of activities that can help you structure your operational employee-centric activities.

Checklist

Preparation Steps

- Assess your IT operations team on
  - IT Operations data transparency
    - Document where your operational data is reported and to whom.
    - Identify who has access to it and if it is encompassing all your IT operations key performance indicators.
    - Assess the frequency the data is refreshed.
  - The educational campaigns and activities
    - Capture how many educational campaigns you are running on a monthly/annual basis.
    - Identify the topics covered in these campaigns.
    - Document the concepts you are utilizing and if any are using gamification techniques.
    - Check if any measurement data is captured.
  - Personas
    - Review your currently defined personas.
    - Assess if they are effectively used within the team.
  - Productivity transparency
    - Identify which improvement activities and productivity measures are regularly released to the organization and all employees.

Problem-Solving Steps

- Develop an employee-centric IT Operations dashboard. This dashboard should include

  - Easy-to-understand and transparent key performance indicators that you believe your employees require to see. Some suggestions are

    - Health of your applications and networks

    - Major incidents and actions

    - Gamification campaigns and improvement actions underway

    - Restrictions currently in place due to certain issues

  - Allow your data to be filtered on department and country levels.

  - Ensure that all your personas can benefit from the data shared.

  - Include both qualitative and quantitative data.

- Design and implement a gamification campaign:

  - Define three business goals you want your IT operations team to drive toward the employees (more will complicate the concept and will increase the possibility of it to fail).

  - Identify the target areas your employees are struggling with in relation to

    - Their behavior toward IT operations as well as their emotions. Choose one only that you need to tackle per business goal.

    - Identify the impact you are seeking, and I suggest you choose two business goals for the short term (show improvements) and one for the long term.

    - I suggest you start with individual-level mechanics and develop to group or collective as you mature.

  - At all stages, keep the data flowing effectively and transparently on your IT operations dashboard.

- Define/redefine your current personas and reduce them to no more than seven (ideally four):

    - Make sure all your IT operations activities, including data, communication, and planning, are taking the personas into consideration.

    - Educate your IT operations team about personas, their benefit, and their use.

- Relentlessly communicate about our IT operations commitment and delivery of productivity measures, improvements, and drive of wider business goals.

Prevention Steps

- Include a "focus" group of employees in your IT operations dashboard review to keep the pressure on your team who the ultimate user is.

- Celebrate the gamification results for both best employees as well as best IT operations team member.

- Get your business management to acknowledge IT operations productivity contribution in global town halls and communications.

Summary

IT operations has a difficult challenge in weighing on deciding between effectively managing the IT landscape and ensuring the "lights are on" while keeping the employees engaged and happy, and in the center of what they do. However, at this age, you can't afford not being employee-centric as it will automatically reflect badly on your daily activities and your team's motivation and will have the ultimate impact on the overall business.

I believe with the right transparency on data, right concentration on personas, and using gamification as a vehicle, your employees will engage and acknowledge the great work your IT operations team does.

Winning the Transformation

The FiReControl Project was initiated by the department for communities and local government in March 2004 in the United Kingdom to integrate 46 stand-alone fire department control rooms into nine regional centers. The project aimed to replace the Fire and Rescue Services' local control rooms across England with purpose-built regional control centers linked by a new IT system.

FiReControl had the objectives of improving national resilience, efficiency, and technology. The department decided on a single, national approach to locally accountable Fire and Rescue Services. The department launched the project too quickly, driven by its broader aims to ensure a better-coordinated response to national disasters, such as terrorist attacks, rail crashes, or floods. The department also wanted to encourage and embed regional government in England. The project's initial plan had a planned cost of £100 million and was to be completed by November 2007.

The project started with new fire control centers constructed and completed while there was considerable delay in awarding the IT contract. Consultants made up over half the management team.

© Mark Ghibril 2023

M. Ghibril, *Employee-Centric IT*, https://doi.org/10.1007/978-1-4842-9186-3_7

Soon after it started, the project started tumbling, and failings came out in every corner of the project. The IT contract was awarded to a company that had no direct experience in supplying the emergency services and that primarily relied on subcontractors over which the department had no visibility or control.

The department rushed the start of the project, failing to follow basic project management. However, the critical area that caused the failure was the lack of consulting, buy-in, and alignment with the Fire and Rescue Services. These local bodies loved their distinctiveness and the freedom they had to choose their equipment. The rationale and benefits of a regional approach were unclear and poorly communicated, and they remained unconvinced. Additionally, the department failed to provide the necessary leadership to make the project successful, overrelying on poorly managed consultants and failing to sort out early problems with delivery by the contractor.

By the time the department took better control on the project, seven years after it had begun, at least £469 million had been wasted, with no IT system delivered and eight of the nine new regional control centers remaining empty and costly to maintain.

The effort was, in the words of the United Kingdom's National Audit Office, "one of the worst cases of project failure" ever seen.

This project is a typical example of many digital transformation projects that have failed. More than 70% of those who failed were due to a lack of proper change management. My experience and many market case studies have proven that technology is almost never the cause of failure in digital transformation programs but a broken or nonexisting change management initiative.

There are multiple frameworks available for defining, implementing, and reinforcing transformational change management activities. These include (but not limited to) the following:

- **The McKinsey 7-S** which breaks down change program into seven components covering strategy, systems and processes, culture, and people

- **Kotter's change management** which has eight steps from creating a sense of urgency to motivate people, communicating with everyone, and defining short-term goals

- **ADKAR change management** from Prosci which starts with awareness and takes you through desire, knowledge, ability, and reinforcement

Based on my experience leading many change management programs in the IT and digital transformation program, I believe the "must-have" ingredients for any change management program for any digital transformation are these:

- **Priming**: Understand why change is necessary

- **Change Impact Analysis**: Identify the change impact on all the different personas

- **Change Road Map**: Provide a transparent journey for implementing the change

- **Train the Trainer**: Train your "maverick" employees to become the testers of your new technology but also your multipliers in the organization

- **Communications**: Report on the progress every minute

Figure 7-1. Key ingredients for change management

In my perspective, reinforcement in the IT world is automatically happening when IT operations take over the technology and continue with their education and communication.

We will tackle each of these ingredients and learn better why these activities are a must if you ever want to succeed in your transformation activities.

Priming

Poor dietary choices, such as overconsumption of energy-dense foods and low intakes of fruit and vegetables, have been associated with an increased risk of noncommunicable diseases (NCDs) such as obesity, type II diabetes, and ischemic heart diseases. In 2017, according to the World Health Organization, NCDs accounted for 90% of all disease-related deaths in Denmark.

The public health department wanted to tackle this issue differently as the previous information campaigns, legislations, and education for the last decade didn't achieve the change needed.

Researchers from Aalborg University and the University of Copenhagen in Denmark initiated an experiment to tackle this challenge.

Eighty-eight participants were recruited in Copenhagen in a Foodscape Lab reproducing a natural lunch situation with a self-serving buffet. The participants weren't informed about the overall study purpose, and the food served was similar to what you find in campus canteens. The experiment ran for 11 days, and the food was provided free of charge with no other incentives.

Participants were recruited through social media, advertisement posters, and the website forsoegsperson.dk (a website specializing in trial volunteers).

The participants were both men and women between 18 and 55 years of age.

The participants participated twice in a controlled setting and another in an experimental one and were assigned in a random, balanced manner.

The experimental setting consisted of a leafy environment with green plants and an odor of herbs. In contrast, the control setting had the salad preportioned into a bowl containing 200g of vegetables. The third experimental setting had divided the premixed salad into each of its components to increase the visual variety of vegetables, yet not providing an actual increase in items.

The outcome was fascinating. The serving and the visual variety of vegetables and the environment have effectively promoted the increased consumption of vegetables compared to energy-dense food.

The researchers used the concept of "priming" to drive this behavior change. Priming is a by-product of subconscious cues that affect how we behave. Priming uses subtle cues and exposes one stimulus to influence a response to a subsequent stimulus without conscious guidance or intention.

Believe it or not, in digital, IT, or any transformation you conduct within the organization, if you want to start the "snowball" effect, you will need to start with applying "priming" concepts to bring the employees to understand, engage, and accept the change.

In IT, my experience has taught me that "outside" consultants, research firms, and "best practices" cannot be used to prime the organization for the needed IT transformation. Instead, you should leverage the insiders in your organization for that priming. Insiders will be more listened to, trusted, and indirectly become your change agents. Insiders are

- Business and IT strategy people who usually work together in defining the key projects that drive business value. They are the ones that should highlight the explicit goals of why business transformation is needed at this moment.

- Leadership team, a combination of your CIO, CDO, and CEO that continuously shares thoughts on where we stand today and the business's good points and possible pain points, priming the positive behavior toward change across the organization.

- IT ambassadors/influencers, usually tech-savvy users, feel the pain in their daily work and know that IT transformation will transform their daily work.

Priming should be very quickly followed by the "awareness" of the change and publicly make the case of why the change is needed and the goals of that IT transformation to instill the priming quickly into everyone's mind.

Change Impact Analysis

In 1998, Amy Wolfson, Ph.D., and Mary Carskadon, Ph.D., ran a study on more than 3000 high school students. They have surveyed these students and compared the survey results to their academic performance. In addition, a study at the University of Minnesota was running an experiment on the start times of school and their impact on high school academic performance.

The preceding two studies and several more had concluded that longer sleep for high school students (more generic teens) had contributed positively to their performance and mood, and fewer reported depressive feelings when they got more sleep.

The consensus was that by changing the school start time by as little as 30 minutes, so instead of 8:00 to 8:30/8:40, the results were tremendous.

The studies also identified that both parents and schools support these findings. However, there has still been massive resistance to change. The resistance was puzzling to researchers that even parents, who want the best for their kids, were hesitant to change.

Another set of studies then concluded that the change wasn't yet possible, not because of the reason and desire for the positive needed change, but another completely unrelated topic:

- The benefits for the students' mental and physical health were clashing with the parents and school administrative and work schedules.

- Studies found that if a school district changes the start times to 08:30, parents will not be able to drive their kids to school and get to work on time.

- Parents with multiple kids have to make different drop-off times.

- Later school times require parents to let teens either get ready and go to school by themselves or be late to work.

- Another issue is that the districts were worried about bus schedules and other transportation logistics, drop-off times, and increased congestions.

- Finally, extracurricular activities covering multiple ages might be impacted or have to push such activities to later in the day.

- Teachers worried they would need to work longer with different times for teens and other classes.

Even though only about 15% of US public high schools now start at 08:30 am or later, this has been the norm in many countries like Finland, Japan, New Zealand, etc., and all of which outperformed the United States on international student achievements.

So why is it still an issue to apply this change in the United States? It is acknowledged by the parents, the teachers, the schools, and the government. Simple: The change impact and the actions to resolve for different stakeholders haven't been appropriately performed. The issue is no longer whether policies promoting later school start times should be adopted, but rather how they should be implemented.

The preceding examples apply 100% to why many transformations fail and lack support. Usually, and after priming and awareness, acknowledging the needed change is reached many times. However, it is crucial to analyze how will this change impact the employees, how will it be applied, and if both can fit the employee's expectation.

To achieve this, two key activities need to happen for any IT change:

- **Stakeholder Analysis**: As the title says, a detailed stakeholder analysis is essential to understand who is involved, impacted, and benefits from the change. As per the students' example, it is insufficient to look at only the directly affected stakeholders and their closer network. For example, an IT change of an ERP system cannot only look at the finance team. It has to understand the impact on the finance team network of collaborators, internal and external, as if they are not supporting the change or not on board, the use of the new tool will be abysmal.

- **Change Impact Analysis**: Here, this activity needs to compare the change for each stakeholder and the impact it has on three areas:

  - Their current processes

  - Their current tools/technology

  - Their current people/network

  - It has to compare it to the new landscape. Then the change will bring and identify the change level (low, medium, high), the impact, and the actions to be taken to minimize or increase the understanding of how this change will be applied.

Change impact is a time-consuming and resourceful activity. However, experience showed me that if you do it well, the rest of the transformation has a much higher percentage of success. The cost at a later stage for an IT transformation without change impact is at least two times more.

Change Road Map

In 2014, 1824 drivers (1362 males and 462 females) in Qatar participated in a survey about the behaviors of driving and skills. The participants were divided between four-wheel drive car drivers and two-wheel drive car drivers.

The survey questionnaire had multiple sections covering sociodemographic information such as age, gender, marital status, educational level, information on driving experience, type of car, frequency of seat belt use and reasons for not wearing a seat belt, speed choice on different roads, and traffic offenses and history of accident during the last three years.

The outcome was very interesting. The drivers of four-wheel drive cars are at higher risk of crashes compared to the drivers of small cars. In addition, they have significantly more traffic violations. This shows that the perceived list is less, and while in fact the car is safer (and usually bigger), the people are not changing their habits and even assuming they are in a more safer environment.

This applies to IT transformations where your outcome might not be what you expected if you don't have a clear checkpoint along your journey.

This is where the change road map comes into play. It should provide the overview of the change coming ahead, painting the big picture as well as the ultimate outcome. The change road map should as well provide key milestones during the journey that can have a clear visible experience to your employees.

Last but not least, your change road map should also identify key milestones for reflection and lessons learned, to allow you always to improve along the way rather than push to the end and ultimately see that your desired outcome has not been achieved.

Train the Trainer

In public health, a study about trainee-led courses was conducted in four states in the United States (Indian, Colorado, Nebraska, and Kansas) covering 317 participants who participated in the last three years. The study was based on an online survey and wanted to examine the outcomes achieved among the participants of courses led by professional trainers vs. trained state-level faculty.

Based on more than 50% response rate, the survey measured the frequency of use of materials, resources, and other skills or tools from the course as well as benefits from attending the course.

The study findings highlighted that both set of respondents (those trained by professional trainers and those trained by train-the-trainer state-based faculty) agreed that they acquired knowledge about the new subject and allowed them to apply the improved abilities to their daily work. The most common reasons for not using the course content as much as intended were due to not having enough time, other staff/peers' lack of training, and not enough funding for continued training.

What were different in the results were the percentages of agreeing of the acquired new knowledge and adaptations to local needs. The train-the-trainer respondents had 10% increase in agreeing or strongly agreeing they had acquired new knowledge and 11% increase in relation to adapting content to local needs.

The findings of this study and many more confirm that train-the-trainer is an effective method for broadly disseminating knowledge. Train-the-trainer is as well less costly than the other traditional methods and allows for courses to be tailored to local content.

Train-the-trainer programs are excellent in IT with many advantages:

- Ability to reach larger number of employees
- Have contextual and local content added to standard content to reach and engage employees better
- Enhance collaboration between IT and business

One main challenge in the train-the-trainer program based on research and my experience is not many replicate the sessions on the local level after a few months when the activity is completed. This can be resolved by providing an online self-learning platform that can be regularly refreshed with content, and the train-the-trainer can use it for keeping up with the information as well as use it as a supporting platform for their sessions for those who want access to info.

Communications

During the 2018–2019 academic year at the three Spanish universities based in Galicia, 600 students from different years and from different fields, covering both science (e.g., mathematics, engineering, economics) and humanities (e.g., journalism, sociology, political science) fields, took part in a large climate change survey. The survey's goal was to understand better the imbalance between the public awareness and knowledge regarding climate change at the same time about a concrete aspect of the weather jet stream.

The student population was chosen on purpose as they are young, educated people who use several sources of information and who belong to one of the generations that will suffer the most from the consequences of the increase in global temperature. Galicia was chosen as the researchers identified that between 1951 and 2017, there were nine episodes of drought to a region that has an economy and way of life that depends on rainfall, and therefore the impact on climate change is quite real. Finally, there is a column in the *La Voz de Galicia*, the third most read newspaper in Spain, called Historias del Tiempo – the Weather Stories format (a pun in Spanish that plays on the words "time" and "weather" as well as "stories" and "histories"). The researchers have been maintaining a special format of information sharing since September 2018, both in press and web formats, and recently covering the topic of jet stream.

The survey had two outcomes that have a huge impact on how communications can be effectively contextualized for nonspecialist audiences, so it builds knowledge rather than concern only.

The first outcome confirmed outcomes also from other research, and those key outcomes are as follows:

- People are aware of the "climate crisis," but this awareness is not leading to change in behavior.

- People remain mostly unfamiliar with the technicalities of the climate change.

- People rely on mass media and journalists rather than from scientific journals or scientists/experts.

The second outcome which is specific to the jet stream topic had a slightly different outcome:

- Higher knowledge was experienced using the special format regarding the jet stream.

- People learned some scientific information rather than pure awareness of a topic.

- Continuous dissemination of complex information in such a format provides better learning for the people and empowers them.

That research gathered characteristics of communications that can effectively deliver highly complex issues for better consumption and understanding. These include the following:

- **Daily Content**: Delivery of daily content on the complex topic.

- **Scientific Dissemination**: Presentation of topics in simple language and supported by graphic material.

- **Historic Perspective**: Providing the relevance of the topic and its evolution in time. It also provides an understanding that the future might have unexpected outcomes.

- **The Importance of Teleconnections**: Providing transparency of connections of different concepts is important to allow linking the right information together.

- **Specialization**: Multidisciplinary science teams can work together and collaborate to provide a communication "experience."

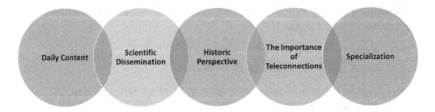

Figure 7-2. Transformational communication characteristics

This study is an excellent example of how IT transformation must communicate such complex, long-winded, and high-impact transformational activities and change to have best consumption by all employees across your organization. Your IT transformation communication should be conducted as follows:

- **Daily Content**: IT should create a communicative social experience by providing very frequent information (ideally daily but latest on a weekly basis) for employees about the transformation to learn about both the transformation and the change impacting them. With this regular content, the employees are learning and contrasting day after day, establishing a trusting relationship with you and the transformational change. In addition, the regular delivery of information constitutes reliability which also is important to build trust with your employees.

- **Scientific Dissemination**: Transformation journeys and concepts in IT have an obvious scientific dissemination purpose. Therefore, your goal should be that your employees incorporate the concepts into their daily work and improve their literacy on how such transformations are positively going to affect their daily work. Therefore, your communications should start way before the transformation activity happens and long after it is completed, providing context and broader knowledge.

- **Historic Perspective**: The journey and evolution of your IT transformation have to be provided to your employees to understand the relevance of the transformation to their work and activities. In addition, your communications should frame the concepts in a department-relevant context so they can relate to it.

- **The Importance of Teleconnections**: Your IT transformation and change communications should emphasize and convey the connections between the different activities and outcomes in an effort to provide a 360 view about the topic toward your employees.

- **Specialization**: Different IT transformation and change teams should collaborate with other departments and employees to bring specialized information that reflect details on the impact the employees will have on a detailed level. This collaboration makes the information thorough and responds to many of the demands of the employees that they need to know: "How does this impact me?" and "What is in it for me?"

Self-Assessment

To self-assess your IT transformation, you need to shift your assessment from technical implementation to change management. Start with assessing:

- Do you have a clear ownership of change management activities within your IT projects and across the entire organization?

    - Do you anchor change management in programs and projects formally or just leave it to those involved to assess what is needed?

- Do you adopt and build insiders within your organization to drive the change with you?

- Do you conduct a thorough stakeholder analysis to understand the impact of change on your stakeholders and personas from process, technology, and people perspective?

- Do you have a road map for change and the change management activities as a mandatory outcome for all your transformation efforts/programs?

- Do you run an extensive knowledge program by educating and training your insiders on the technology, its use cases, and how it can be beneficial to your employees?

- Do you engage at all time through various channels and continuously demonstrate the progress you are achieving in your transformational activities?

If you have all these, then the success of your transformation activities and getting your employees on board will be significantly higher. If you have done some informal change management activities or don't know how to anchor it now with all your activities that are running in parallel, then follow the following checklist.

Checklist

Preparation Steps

- Assess your IT transformation employee-centricity through

    - Understanding which change management activities are taking place in which programs you are running

- Initiating feedback from employees at current or already completed transformation programs to capture what they have perceived worked and didn't work. Ensure to capture here feedback on

  - Activities that were taken to prime for the change

  - Change impact analysis activities (if done at all or not) and their outcomes

  - Change road map and its clarity on milestones

  - Educational steps taken along the transformation

  - Communication and transparency of the transformation and the change it brought

- Identifying if you already have the skills and talent that can drive the change management activities or not

Problem-Solving Steps

To succeed in your continuous transformation within IT and digital and drive employee-centricity, I suggest you perform these activities (at a minimum):

- Provide a combination of digital and face-to-face interactions across the organization regarding the need for change and personalize it toward the stakeholders and personas you are talking with.

- Use storytelling to gain employee buy-in and organization traction for transformation initiatives. Narratives should be studied carefully to ensure the context and delivery is fitting.

- Put in place a community of insiders who will be your change agents that can facilitate the change process, distribute knowledge by ensuring those who get stuck get the help they need, and ensure collective energy are spent toward the transformation journey:

  - Ask them to drive the messages across all physical and virtual channels to amplify the transformational benefit and their support and commitment to the journey.

  - Senior management should lead by example by practicing engagement. For example, giving simple comments or "liking" the posts on internal social networks is a very powerful way to show their support.

- Run as early as possible your change impact analysis:

  - Stakeholder analysis is vital to understand who is impacted with the change and their role in your IT transformation.

  - Utilize methods such as design thinking to ensure all impacted employees are involved as well as understanding the different roles and stages employees might be at during the change life cycle.

- Knowledge boosting along the journey is a must, even if the transformation is not major. Ensure you

  - Create a learning repository including a self-documenting area to allow everyone to contribute to the lessons learned and best practices along the digital transformation timeline.

  - Bring the commitment among leaders across the entire organization to allow time to all employees to spend on educating themselves about the change from a perspective of

    - Awareness on the impacted processes and their roles within the process

    - Ease in using the new functionalities/technology

    - Interaction points with other employees in the new way of working

- Spend effort on continuous communications along the entire journey through

  - Creating an online community to allow everyone to see what's happening, when, and why.

  - Empowering of employees to be able to express themselves, contribute, and get involved. The employees need to feel that the change is a shared purpose, and this is identical at all levels of the organization.

Prevention Steps

- Stop any transformation activity that doesn't have change management ingrained in it. Even though you might be pushed in the short term to achieve productivity or cost measures, digital transformation without a proper change management will reduce your entire organization productivity for the future.

- Ensure you have a lean change framework on a program level and everyone in your IT organization is educated about it.

- Continuously review the change management activities, identifying what works for your employees, what needs improving, and what is missing. Don't wait for the project to be done to review. I recommend you do a review on the program and overall level of your change management efforts on a quarterly basis.

Summary

In current times, digital technology is a driving force of change and digital transformation programs across almost all companies. In addition, digital technology is evolving in an unprecedented pace. The challenge for organizations is to successfully run digital projects as part of their digital transformation programs while addressing the changes required for their leadership, talents, and employees to embark and support their digital journey.

Ensuring your IT teams drive transformation projects not as pure technology but as a way of employee-centric enhanced interaction will only be the way to succeeding. Remember that even though employees might interact with relative ease with similar digital technologies in their personal life, this differs hugely in a work environment.

My experience and research show that change management is by far the most enduring bottleneck to digital projects and transformation. Doing it correctly and efficiently will ensure your IT organization can succeed in your transformation efforts and ensure you win your employees' trust along the journey.

Winning the Innovation

In the early 1970s, a little startup called "Southwest Airlines" was facing a turbulent time. They were consistently losing money, posting a net loss of $1.6 million by 1972, and were forced to sell one of its planes.

Southwest had to find a solution. One of the ideas that came up by the ground operations teams was to unload and load passengers than other airlines so the planes could be back in the air more often.

The concept they called the "10-minute turn" meant the passengers and baggage were unloaded, the plane cleaned and restocked, and new passengers got on, all in the ten-minute window. This was an unrealistic goal since most airlines took almost an hour to turn a plane.

All hands were needed to get the plane out of the gate, and this meant it required everyone to support this crazy idea, and innovative ways of working had to be found to save the company and the employees' jobs.

Everyone went beyond their regular duties. Pilots volunteered to work the ramps to understand better what the rampers do. Flight attendants were helping with cleaning and anything that could initiate ideas for improvements.

© Mark Ghibril 2023

M. Ghibril, *Employee-Centric IT*, https://doi.org/10.1007/978-1-4842-9186-3_8

The process and improvements were tried, improved, and worked on repeatedly until they achieved this big audacious goal. Although Southwest was not always able to turn planes in ten minutes, the quick turnarounds happened enough to make the policy successful and make Southwest's revenue and profits positive.

With all the security regulations, increased carry-on luggage, and amount of people flying, Southwest still has the fastest turn time in the industry at around 25 minutes.

The preceding story is a prime example of an innovation culture that fosters and encourages creative thoughts at all levels of the organization to achieve market-leading solutions to problems.

In organizations, innovation can take two forms:

- **Incremental Innovation**: Series of small improvements made to a company's existing products or services. Usually, these are created using existing knowledge and resources within the company. Incremental innovation will still require understanding the problem at hand to differentiate you from the competition. Incremental innovation can be continuous to always develop improved products and solutions based on insights from markets and customers.

- **Radical Innovation**: Introducing brand-new products or services that replace existing ones or completely new to the market. Usually, companies require new knowledge and resources to build and release radical innovations to the market as it's a big step from what they are doing to date. Radical innovation is usually noticeable and visible and quite occasional as it is usually time and cost intensive to develop a brand-new solution.

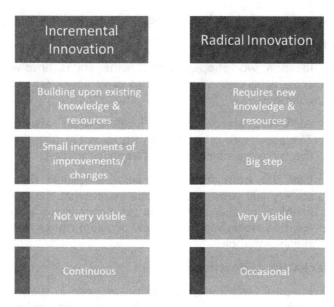

Figure 8-1. Incremental vs. radical innovation

The Southwest Airlines story provides a few essential aspects that can be and should be copied into IT innovation:

- Successful innovation only works if you have an apparent problem defined that you need to resolve. IT is an enabler to the business and therefore utilizes insights from your organization and employees to drive your innovation.

- Innovation is not always a brand-new product, solution, or technology. I see a lot of effort is put in finding the next IT homegrown solution to an apparent problem. My experience showed me that small increments of improvements have way more impact on your organization than big steps, especially as an internal IT function. Of course, in the digital space, radical innovation sometimes is needed, but don't put all your eggs in one basket.

- One department alone cannot innovate, especially in IT. You need all people involved in the process to engage, give feedback, and contribute. These are your employees, your delivery partners, and your organization's customers.

To do that, you can apply the following tools that worked for me:

- **Ideation workshops**
  - Ideation workshops, as the name states, involve cross-departmental activities to drive new ideas and solutions.
  - ALWAYS start this with a "Reverse Brain" activity. The activity does not begin with ideas but identifies the current problems around a particular topic.
  - Like the story from Southwest, a Reverse Brain activity will allow you to hone in on what the real problem is and enable you to concentrate your ideation workshop on the real problem rather than the assumed one.

- **Hackathons/ideathons**
  - Multiday activities that work around a specific problem and find the actual minimum viable product of a solution to the problem.
  - With Gartner highlighting that more than 40% of employees are now business technologists, technology savvy, or experienced technologists with business roles rather than IT roles, your hackathons can surprise you with the ideas, MVPs, and solutions you can get when you combine the power of many.

Self-Assessment

Winning the innovation is both exciting and daunting in IT organizations. To assess your maturity on IT innovation, assess yourself using the following questions:

- Do you have a culture of innovation that encourages cross-departmental collaboration on IT challenges/problems?
- Do your IT employees drive ideation workshops or hackathons by themselves to achieve solutions for their problems?
- Have you recently released an incremental or radical innovation to your employees?

If you had done all these, then you have a great culture to be proud of. If not and you need some help, the checklist will give you some direction.

Checklist

Preparation Steps

- Assess your IT innovation through

    - Understanding the methods and means your team is using today to innovate

    - Understanding the level of collaboration with departments outside IT and your partners to initiate new ideas, concepts, and solutions

    - Identifying the level of innovation you had so far and the success it delivered

Problem-Solving Steps

IT innovation is not a top-down activity. Therefore, you need your entire IT organization to be part of such a culture of creative thought and drive. To achieve it, I suggest you perform the following:

- Provide the space and time for your IT teams to think. I suggest you allow 10% to 20% of your team member's time to be freed up from day-to-day work.

- Instill the culture of "collaborative innovation" supporting and nudging your team to collaborate with each other and with other departments on problems the employees are facing or insights that need to be tackled.

- If you have a major challenge to solve, don't leave it to the 10% time of your employees, dedicate the right resources for 100% of the time to tackle it quickly and efficiently.

- Ensure your team knows that incremental innovation is as important (if not more) as radical innovation, and therefore every step of improvement is a success.

- Run a hackathon once a year to drive parallel concepts to a large challenge, while run as many ideation workshops as you need.

Prevention Steps

- Train your team members on effective ideation workshop moderation and dedicate a team that manages the hackathons.

- Celebrate every small improvement as much as the radical one.

Summary

IT can only achieve employee-centricity with continuous incremental innovation and some occasional radical innovation. Fostering IT innovation not as a return on investment (ROI) of IT spending but real measures of introducing small incremental improvements provides a competitive edge to the organization, while it also instills creative leadership within IT.

Collaborative innovation with the rest of your organization proves IT organizations' employee-centricity and will support to win the minds of their employees. As much as cost savings and operational stability are important, IT innovation will shoot up your employee satisfaction and engagement to the highest levels.

Winning Your IT Team

In Mumbai, the most successful and biggest food delivery business is not Uber Eats, Deliveroo, or many similar startups in India like Swiggy and Runner. It is the dabbawalas of Mumbai.

The dabbawalas of Mumbai have been delivering food for almost 125 years. The dabbawalas of Mumbai are made out of 5000 self-managed, semiliterate workers. They deliver around 130,000 lunches from customers' homes to their offices daily with astonishing reliability, precision, and efficient cost. In 2010, a study by the Harvard Business School identified that the dabbawalas make fewer than 3.4 mistakes per million transactions, meaning less than 400 delayed or missing lunches in a year.

The dabbawalas consist of small units of 25 people each to ensure low-cost service. The tight schedule of the train lines regulated everyone's work. Lunchboxes have to reach the client by 13:00 every day, and it can take up to three hours to deliver them. The dabbawalas' built-in buffer capacity ensures thin margins of error, and each unit has extra workers who fill wherever needed. Each dabbawala has a single collection and delivery area. They tour their neighborhood on foot or by bicycle at mid-morning, collecting an average of 30 customer lunchboxes. These are sorted at a local office or railway station, and each dabbawala gets on a train heading for their delivery area. On arrival, all lunchboxes are sorted again before being loaded onto bicycles and handcarts for the final delivery.

Dabbawalas have a very high commitment to their job. They are very well trained, they are paid excellent salaries compared to other jobs for semiliterate labor, and they receive recognition and respect within their organization and the community they serve. A dabbawala is well trained and empowered. The organization is run as a cooperative, and all dabbawalas are equal partners with supervisors called mukadams, who are democratically elected. Finally, many dabbawalas worship Vithala, a Hindu god who teaches that giving food is a great virtue. They have an emotional bond, which promotes a high degree of trust and cooperation.

The success of dabbawalas was studied by Harvard Business School, and the critical pillars for their success were identified as organization management, their processes, and their culture.

The dabbawalas show that even ordinary workers can achieve the extraordinary with the proper structure, system, and culture. Even Richard Branson has spent a day learning their secrets.

The story of dabbawalas shows technology isn't the solution for excellent service and customer-centricity and satisfaction. Technology can be purely an additional enabler for such things; however, the organization structure, processes, and culture make any team succeed. And IT teams are not different.

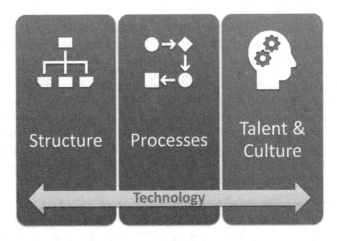

Figure P4-1. Team success pillars

To get your IT team to become employee-centric and reach excellence, they will need to adapt many dabbawalas excellence. You will need to work with your team and win your team's structure and management, processes, and internal team talent and culture. All three pillars need to be perfectly aligned and mutually reinforcing.

In Chapter 9, we will tackle the IT team's structure, followed by IT processes in Chapter 10, and complete this part with talent and culture in Chapter 11.

Winning the IT Team's Structure

Today, the Cleveland Clinic is an exemplary hospital for a patient-centric and employee-centric institution with world-class customer care executives from all over the world to come and learn how they achieved this.

However, this was not always the case. In 2009, in the US government survey on hospital performances, the Clinic's overall score was average that year. Its performance was in the bottom percentile in areas of patient-centricity, which includes staff responsiveness, room cleanliness, and doctors' and nurses' communications. "Patients were coming to us for the clinical excellence, but they did not like us very much," CEO Cosgrove says. And from stories he'd heard from patients and their families and the personal stories of employees themselves, he decided to drive a transformation to achieve experience excellence worthy of all patients. Cosgrove explained that the transformation needs to shift the care delivery group to become caregivers.

Cosgrove and his team had to tackle two main problems:

- Doctors and nurses typically focus on performing procedures and treatments but often fail to explain them in terms patients can understand.

- Employees are unaware of the patients' survey scores and bad scoring and don't believe they matter that much or don't understand how to improve the patient experience.

© Mark Ghibril 2023
M. Ghibril, *Employee-Centric IT*, https://doi.org/10.1007/978-1-4842-9186-3_9

To make the patient experience a strategic priority, employees had to understand what it meant and what each person's responsibility for delivering it entailed exactly. Cosgrove and his team defined a broad, holistic definition: the patient experience was everyone and everything people encountered from the time they decided to go to the Clinic until they were discharged. The effort to improve it became known as "managing the 360."

Cosgrove created an Office of Patient Experience, including project managers, data experts, and service excellence trainers. Their responsibilities include conducting and analyzing patient surveys, interpreting patients' complaints, administering "voice of the patient" advisory councils, training employees, and working with units to identify and fix problems.

At most hospitals, the primary relationship is between the doctor and the patient; the rest of the staff members see themselves in supporting roles. But in the eyes of patients, all their interactions are essential.

To get a feeling of a patient's experience, the Cleveland Clinic asked a woman undergoing an uncomplicated colorectal surgery to keep a journal of everyone who cared for her during her five-day stay. It turned out that there were eight doctors, 60 nurses, and so many others. Moreover, her journal did not even consider employees in administrative areas such as billing, food, and parking – people who did not interact directly with her but might have significantly impacted her stay. This highlighted a big realization and confirmation that all employees are caregivers and that a caregiver-centric one should replace the doctor-centric relationship.

First, the Clinic adopted a new care model to improve collaboration, increase quality and efficiency, and reduce costs. It transformed from a traditional hospital structure, in which a department of medicine supervises specialties such as cardiology and gastroenterology. In contrast, a surgery department oversees general surgery and cardiac, transplant, and other specialty procedures. Instead, it created institutes where multidisciplinary teams treat all the conditions affecting a particular organ system. For example, its heart and vascular institute now includes everything concerning the heart and circulatory systems, and cardiologists and surgeons see patients together. The new model had positive effects not only on quality and costs but also on the patient experience.

To further improve the patient experience, the Cleveland Clinic introduced a new concept of dividing tasks between the central campus and the community center. This decentralization resulted in higher patient satisfaction and higher satisfaction among the physicians themselves.

Then, to get everyone in the organization to start thinking and acting accordingly, they ran a half-day exercise for all 43,000 employees. All participated as caregivers, sharing stories about what they did – and what they could do better – to put the patient first. They were also trained in basic behaviors practiced by workers at exemplary service organizations: active listening to and assisting patients, building rapport, and thanking them.

The program was launched in late 2010. It took a full year for everyone to go through it, and as hoped, the program had a profound impact. All employees, physicians, and nonphysicians were amazed by the experience of sitting together as caregivers. Participants shared frustrations about not always being able to provide a nurturing environment. Even doctors who had been skeptical about the exercise felt it was worthwhile.

Cleveland Clinic's story highlights the importance of the vision, structure, roles, and responsibility in any organization that would like to be employee- and customer-centric.

For your IT organization, this can be done by

- **Vision and Mission**: Employee-centricity has to be ingrained in your vision and mission. The entire IT organization has to understand the importance of being obsessed with serving the employees. This isn't the role of one department in IT but every single person.

- **Structure**: To perform their work most efficiently and be employee-centric, you will need to have a team that provides the tools to help all other IT employees to use, refer to, and get training and direction on continuous improvement to be better employee-centric. They will need to be the "voice of the employee" in every decision, implementation, and adoption foreseen.

- **Responsibilities**: You will need to support cross-departmental teams with end-to-end responsibility for IT products and services, including their full employee-centric delivery. These groups are not bound to an organization or department but work together to improve the employee-centric activities. Each employee has to understand their role's contribution to the employee-centric vision. All of them have a role to play in building relationships and trusting ones. All employees are encouraged to seek improvements in employee-centricity, even if it is not in their specific area of responsibility.

- **Attitudes**: Employees must take time to interact with other employees to share information about upcoming changes, discuss issues, and identify areas of improvement.

- **Knowledge**: Employees must be cross-trained in different activities to allow them to step in in terms of crisis or challenging transformations to help and keep the entire organization employee-centric.

Figure 9-1. IT organization important elements

Self-Assessment

I have seen that IT organizations call themselves employee-centric but rarely are reflected in their structure, vision and mission, and execution. Therefore, here are a few assessment questions that can help you if your IT organization is winning the IT structure:

- Do you clearly articulate the employee-centricity characteristics in the vision and mission statements of your entire IT organization?

- Do you set in your working principles employee-facing functions and supporting functions that all have the same targets around employee-centricity?

- Do you have a center of excellence that is continuously finding improvements to be adopted and implemented by every IT employee to make them champions of employee-centricity?

- Do you review performance purely on technical objectives achieved or also around the way of working and attitudes related to employee-centricity and care?

- Do you cross-pollinate your team and train them regularly on other aspects in your IT organization for everyone to be able to understand each other's roles and drive employee-centricity as one team rather than a scattered group?

If you perform all these, you are one of the very few top percentile organizations that have an IT structure that is employee-centric. It is not easy and not very common; however, you will have next a checklist that will help you drive in that direction.

Checklist

Preparation Steps

- Assess your IT employees' understanding of employee-centricity through

  - Recording the understanding of your IT employees on what employee-centricity means to them.

  - Identifying any data you currently capture that can capture the employee-centric maturity. This includes surveys, complaints, support tickets, project/program lessons learned, and any other data from focus groups that were conducted.

  - Analyzing the relationship between the employees and your IT department to understand who and how your IT employees engage with the employees.

Problem-Solving Steps

- As Simon Sinek says, start with Why and compel your entire IT employees to understand that employee-centricity is a strategic topic for all, and this can be done as follows:

  - Get a clear definition of what employee-centricity means to your IT organization.

  - You can achieve this by getting representatives from each of your teams to work on this definition and ensure commitment that they all can stand behind that vision/definition.

- Make employee-centricity ingrained in the employees' objectives and key results and assess their progress on a regular basis.

- Ask employees from your organization to share their experiences with the entire IT organization. You can do this either in your employee town halls or part of a set of activities around employee-centricity. Utilize these channels to highlight to the entire organization the need that all IT employees must be employee-centric and the relationship with the rest of the organization employees is not only concentrated to the few with employee-facing roles but for each and every one.

- Revisit your IT structure and adopt an improved setup that should have at least the following criteria:

  - Organizational team structures ensure employees who conduct the same activities but for different IT products are joined to share experiences, improve quality, and ensure standards of work. Examples of these teams can be

    - Development and operations

    - Product management

    - Cyber security

    - Business partnering

    - Employee-centricity center of excellence

    - …

  - Employee-centric functional team structures that ensure end-to-end accountability toward the employees for the IT products they use in their daily processes. Examples of these teams can be

    - Customer relationship management

    - Manufacturing

    - Supply chain management

    - …

- Create an employee-centricity center of excellence that regularly assesses the maturity of your entire organization, collects feedback from your employees, and works with each of your organizational and functional teams to drive improvements and increase the level of employee experience.

  - Ensure your IT employees who are in the center of excellence are also part of the functional teams to help always drive the "voice of the employee" in case it is forgotten or missed.

- Define a set of employee-centric attitudes you expect from all your IT employees that runs around the topics already mentioned earlier in the book, such as

  - Listening

  - Caring

  - Communication

  - Collaboration

- Regularly run knowledge-sharing sessions to cross-train and inform your IT employees on what others are doing and how they all are part of the interaction of employees and that they all have a role to play in employee-centricity.

Prevention Steps

- Run regular employee-centricity workshops to share stories about what worked great, what can be improved, and how to always put the employees at the heart of everything you do.

- Ensure you have a lean change framework on a program level and everyone in your IT organization is educated about it.

Summary

The IT organization's decisions on their vision, structure, roles, and responsibilities are essential to their success. Employee-centric organizations can only succeed if they ingrain in every employee's DNA that employee-centricity is part of their day-to-day activities and contributes toward their improved performance, targets, and success. Therefore, winning your IT structure will be based on your IT team being obsessed with serving employees. By providing a structure and tools that support their execution on their obsession and have the knowledge to work together as ONE team toward ONE employee-centric outcome, you will be able to be successful.

CHAPTER

10

Winning the IT Team's Processes

In 1990, Elizabeth Newton of Stanford University ran an experiment with 40 students who were asked to "tap" out well-known songs with their fingers while another group of 40 students tried to name the melodies. Each tapper was partnered up with a listener. Tappers were told to pick a well-known song such as "Happy Birthday" and tap out the rhythm on the table. The listeners were asked to guess the name of the song. Before they started, each tapper was asked to predict how often the listeners would be able to guess the song. The tappers said they expected the listeners would recognize the song about half of the time (50% success rate). Listeners, meanwhile, learned that they were going to be guessing what tune their partner was tapping. They were told to write down their guess after each tune.

After agreeing not to communicate with their partners until the tapping exercise was over, listeners and tappers were brought together! Having tapped all three tunes, tappers were asked to name the first tune they had tapped. The experimenter then told both the listeners and the tappers that she would be tapping out this tune. They were to estimate what percentage

© Mark Ghibril 2023
M. Ghibril, *Employee-Centric IT*, https://doi.org/10.1007/978-1-4842-9186-3_10

of an audience of 100 listeners would be able to name the tune if they heard the tapping amplified in a recital hall.

The outcome was fascinating. Groups overestimated the ability of their partners. Out of the 120 songs tapped, the listeners only guessed 3 songs correctly, a 2.5% success rate. The estimates of the tappers were so wrong because the tappers could hear the melody in their head. They knew the song, which caused them to miscalculate the listener's comprehension.

This experiment coined the term "curse of knowledge." This experiment and further ones in that field identified that the curse of knowledge is the reason why

- Experts have difficulties teaching beginners.
- Team members have difficulties communicating.
- People have difficulties in predicting the behaviors of others.

And in IT, the curse of knowledge is very much prevalent in the daily work and interaction with non-IT-savvy workforce. IT processes are in place to document the knowledge for the steps needed to achieve the outcomes you desire in the most efficient, standardized, and compliant manner. What is forgotten is that knowledge changes but processes are not, and this causes frustration, broken processes, and lack of employee-centricity.

The "curse of knowledge" also causes IT teams to be seen as non-employee-centric; employees struggle with their daily tools and get frustrated with the IT processes (which the IT teams believe are straightforward, simple, and clear).

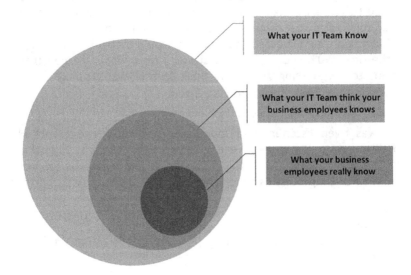

What your IT Team Know

What your IT Team think your business employees knows

What your business employees really know

Figure 10-1. Curse of knowledge in IT organizations

Therefore, to win your IT employees' trust to change and transform to an employee-centric mindset, you must tackle the curse of knowledge, allow it to not manifest, and get it out of their system.

This can be done as follows:

- **Put a prioritization mechanism** that sets the pace, rhythm, and priorities for all IT and employee-centricity at its helm. This mechanism will then be used as the daily checklist for their tasks, prioritizing when you have conflicting tasks and the time allowed for each. This mechanism also synchronizes everyone and imposes discipline in an environment that might be otherwise chaotic.

- **Put a regular feedback mechanism** from the employees and the IT management and peers. IT employees have to identify when they moved away from employee-centricity, why this has happened, and how they can bounce back. They will need to hear it from the organization themselves and their team leaders and colleagues. This can be done through

  - Regular sharing of IT satisfaction survey data in internal meetings

  - IT satisfaction as the target for all IT employees

  - Listening sessions where you invite non-IT employees to share their experiences with daily IT

- **Ensure problems or issues impacting the employee-centricity are dealt with immediately.** This allows no issues to be "swept under the rug" and provides the IT employees with evident empowerment if they see similar behaviors. Like Toyota does in its manufacturing plants, any worker who spots a problem can pull the "cord" to halt a production line, so the issue is addressed immediately.

- **Set employee expectations** on what to expect. This allows them to understand how employees outside IT will be well off if they conform to a particular process, get solutions faster resolved, and ensure their satisfaction.

Self-Assessment

To figure out if you have employee-centric processes, answer these questions:

- Do you have prioritization mechanisms in place in your processes to help your IT teams identify the common employee-centric prioritization for all teams rather than being individualistic?

- Do you regularly review your processes, activities, and data to reflect if your teams are executing in an employee-centric manner?

- Do you empower your IT team members to raise issues impacting your employee-centricity and ensure these are dealt with swiftly?

- Are you setting clear expectations within your organization to what to expect from an IT employee and the attitudes, processes, and activities that drive the employee-centric culture and outcomes?

If you perform all these, then you are on the right track to achieve extraordinary IT experiences for your employees. If not, then let's jump into a checklist that can help you.

Checklist

Preparation Steps

- Assess your IT processes in relation to

    - Criteria for execution that is employee-centric

    - Prioritization criteria that assist your overall organizational objectives as well as your employee's experience and satisfaction

- Assess your IT continuous improvement activities to understand better:

    - What feedback mechanisms you currently conduct within your IT organization and with your employees around current IT processes and activities

    - Activities taken as an outcome of your IT satisfaction survey data, IT support data, and other data sources to improve processes and engagements

    - What issues are raised proactively by your employees that are hindering them to be employee-centric

Problem-Solving Steps

- Start small with selective processes. You can select which processes to start with by

    - Identifying with your employees their biggest frustrations and tackling those processes first. Remember that the curse of knowledge is a fact, and employee perception is reality.

    - Documenting the current process steps (if not properly identified/documented) and identifying the bottlenecks, roadblocks, and issues experienced.

    - Assigning the right IT team (end-to-end view) that needs to be involved to act on these process improvement activities and drive this change effort.

- Involve your employees in the improvement efforts:

    - Map your employee journey within the process.

    - Define the expectations and planned experiences that the employees are looking for, jointly. Some expectations will be unrealistic, and therefore a joint effort to arrive to an achievable outcome is important.

    - Make your employees part of the solution and ensure your IT team members are driving improvements that are employee-centric rather than IT-centric.

    - Implement improvements and monitor your employees' interactions after the improvements to check if you have achieved the outcomes expected.

- Empower and reward your IT employees:

    - In the quest to be more employee-centric, your IT employees need to feel they are empowered to raise issues that are hindering the process to be efficient, successful, and employee-centric.

    - IT employees must be able to feel that they have a big part to play in your employee-centricity journey and that they can influence it, contribute to it, and improve it.

- Measure continuously:
  - Every interaction with your processes will generate some type of data.
  - Define a stringent set of KPIs that concentrate on your employee-centricity as well as the expectations agreed with your employees for that process.
  - Look at all the data based on your employee journey and employee-centricity lens rather than IT lens.
  - Measure and improve continuously.
- Expand:
  - After you have conducted successful improvements in the key set of processes, expand your activities to the rest of your IT processes.

Prevention Steps

- Set regular touchpoints with your organization. These should be listening and feedback on all their touchpoints with the processes and understand the gap between their expectations of the experience and their actual experience.

- Communicate and celebrate the improvements within your IT teams as well as to the entire organization.

Summary

IT organizations achieving employee-centric processes will win their employees' trust, increase their satisfaction, and deliver extraordinary experience. With the enormous level of activities and tasks IT teams are experiencing in this transformational time, prioritization is a must, feedback is essential, and expectation setting is crucial to achieve employee-centricity.

Winning the IT Talent and Culture

In 1977, researchers assigned a chess problem task to randomly allocated participants in two groups. Two sessions were conducted.

In session one, participants of both groups were asked to complete a questionnaire about the amount of time they played chess during the week, the number of years they played, and the enjoyment they got in playing chess. When the participants completed the questionnaire, they were told that the experimenter would enter the information into the computer and that task would take around ten minutes. They were free to do whatever they liked.

The room had chess problem tasks on the table, and some magazines and coffee were made available for the participants if they chose to have them. Before the experimenter left, the experimental group was told that there was a monetary reward for the participants who could work on the chess problems in ten minutes. The reward is only for this session and not the next one. The control group was not offered or mentioned any monetary reward.

© Mark Ghibril 2023
M. Ghibril, *Employee-Centric IT*, https://doi.org/10.1007/978-1-4842-9186-3_11

In session two, both groups had the same information, and the experimental group was reminded that there was no reward for the task this time.

After both sessions, the participants were asked to respond to questionnaires evaluating the task, that is, to what degree they found the task enjoyable. Both groups reported that they found the task interesting.

The results have shown that the experimental group had a significant decrease in time spent on the chess problems from session one to session two compared to the group that wasn't offered any monetary rewards. This study and many similar ones have confirmed that intrinsic motivation is not linked to monetary or other contingent rewards.

This applies strongly to IT employees. The IT talent, which is in huge demand, requires different reward types to keep them engaged and motivated to drive your employee-centricity vision. This applies to both retaining your key talent and attracting new talent.

I believe intrinsic motivation can be fulfilled through collaboration, community, and psychological safety.

Figure 11-1. Fulfilling intrinsic motivation

Collaboration and Community

Steve Wynn, the founder of Wynn Resort and Casino, and his family were staying at Four Seasons in Paris, and they had ordered breakfast in bed. His daughter only ate half of a croissant, leaving the other half for later. Steve and his family left for the day to explore Paris, and when they returned to the hotel room, the croissant was gone. His daughter was disappointed, assuming the housekeeping had gotten rid of it.

On the telephone, there was a message from the front desk. The message said that housekeeping had removed the half-croissant from the room, assuming that the Wynn family would prefer a fresh pastry upon arrival. The front desk contacted the kitchen to set aside a croissant, and they informed room service to deliver the pastry upon request.

This simple action taken by the entire team of Four Seasons made the stay for Steve and his family magical. The level of teamwork and communication between different departments in the hotel was simply outstanding, and all understood the result – customer satisfaction.

The collaboration between the IT team members is also crucial to developing magical employee experiences. Therefore, IT leaders have to

- Recognize their role in nurturing their teams' development to maximize their productivity, creativity, motivation, and collaboration

- Fine-tune their department activities to enable employees to perform and collaborate at optimal levels

- Build the sense of community around employee-centricity and team to keep them motivated, excited, and keen to continue working with a common goal of achieving highest employee satisfaction

Psychological Safety

After years of intensive analysis under the name of Project Aristotle, Google discovered the key to good teamwork.

In 2012, Google kicked off Project Aristotle. The project team analyzed data in more than 100 operational teams at the company for multiple years.

Google's intense data collection led to the one main conclusion: in the best teams, members show sensitivity and, most importantly, listen to one another. Google's findings introduced the core concept of "psychological safety" – a shared belief that the team is safe for interpersonal risk-taking.

The outcome of Google's project highlighted what has been known already: the best teams are mindful that all members should contribute to the conversation equally and respect one another's emotions. It has less to do with who is in a team but more with how the members interact.

To help IT managers achieve psychological safety within their teams, the core elements of motivational interviewing should be applied. Motivational interviewing (MI) offers the steps of psychological safety that they can drive by coaching the employees themselves to find ways to help themselves change, collaborate, and achieve positive outputs.

The core elements of motivational interviewing are evocation, acceptance, and compassion.

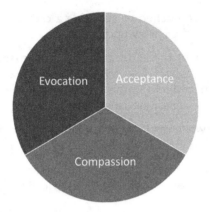

Figure 11-2. Motivational interviewing core elements

- **Evocation**: The idea of motivational interviewing is to allow employees themselves to identify their priorities and explore the reasons for change rather than informing them. The IT leader has to support them to achieve that.

- **Acceptance**: The IT leader takes a nonjudgmental stance, seeks to understand the person's perspectives and experiences, expresses empathy, highlights strengths, and respects a person's right to make informed choices about changing or not changing.

- **Compassion**: The IT leader actively promotes and prioritizes the employee's welfare and well-being in a selfless manner.

To achieve the preceding core elements, the IT leader has to build the core skills of OARS:

- Ask **O**pen-ended questions to draw out and explore the team member's experiences, perspectives, and ideas.

- Use **A**ffirmation of strengths, efforts, and past successes to help build the team member's hopes and confidence in their ability to change.

- Employ **R**eflections based on careful listening and understanding of what the team member would like to achieve. This can be done by repeating, rephrasing, or offering a deeper guess about what the person is trying to communicate.

- Finish by **S**ummarizing to ensure shared understanding and reinforce critical points made by the team member.

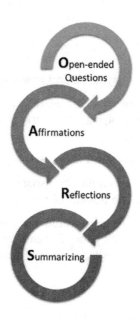

Figure 11-3. OARS

Self-Assessment

IT talent and culture assessment is not straightforward; however, a few questions can help you confirm if you are on track or not:

- Do you purely use extrinsic motivation techniques (e.g., monetary rewards) to reward your IT employees?

- Do you provide a culture that encourages collaboration and sense of community around employee-centricity?

- Do you empower your employees in their roles and department activities to optimally collaborate toward employee-centricity?

- Do your IT leaders utilize some of the core elements of motivational interviewing such as coaching, listening, and compassion with their team members?

If you have most of the preceding questions, then you have the right culture that also attracts and retains the right talent. If not, then follow the checklist to help you drive toward such a goal.

Checklist

Preparation Steps

- Assess your IT performance and rewards model to

  - Capture any intrinsic motivational aspects that you are currently applying and working and which ones you are missing

- Assess your collaboration levels within your teams to

  - Understand if open and transparent collaboration is happening for the benefit of the employee

- Identify if the sense of community toward employee-centricity exists across your IT teams by understanding if your department activities allow and support cross-team collaboration.

Problem-Solving Steps

- Drive a clear message across your IT organization from the top that intrinsic motivation for every employee is the target you drive for now in your yearly performance reviews.

- Ensure all your IT leaders are executing on that goal by rewarding employees through

  - Offering them a higher level of empowerment in their roles

  - Redefining the IT department activities and charters to emphasize on the transparent cross-team collaboration

  - Building a sense of community through community managers leading those within your IT teams and acknowledging that such communities are needed to drive the common goal of employee-centricity across your entire IT organization

- Train all your IT leaders on motivational interviewing and coaching and consistently reemphasize this skill within your succession planning.

Prevention Steps

- Include in all your IT talent development and recruiting activities your emphasis on intrinsic motivations, community buildup, collaboration transparency, and psychological safety.

- Communicate and regularly celebrate those IT employees who are living and breathing these elements internally in IT but also to the wider organization.

- Let your IT leaders be role models on all these aspects, within your IT teams but more importantly toward your wider organization.

Summary

To win the best talent, you will also need to create the best culture. Culture can be driven by senior management however only if the direct supervisors/ IT leaders of your teams are breathing and living that culture. Therefore, nurturing intrinsic motivational aspects of your IT organization will drive a culture of open collaboration, a sense of community and belonging to a common employee-centric goal, and the psychological safety every employee yearns for to perform their very best.

With this chapter, I have covered all the core elements that allow you to build the highest level of trust in your IT organization. If you apply all these core elements, you will win your organization's employees' hearts and minds, allowing them to consistently have extraordinary IT experience which your employees will be grateful for. In the last part of this book, I will share some insights on how you can evangelize these core elements at all levels of your IT teams.

Evangelizing Employee-Centric IT in Your Organization

In 2018, the Programme d'Enseignemet Ciblé (PEC) was introduced to address the learning crisis in Cote d'Ivoire, whereby many children do not acquire essential foundational skills like reading and arithmetic at the right time. Cote d'Ivoire's crisis was significant: only 48% of students achieved sufficient threshold in literacy at the end of primary school and only 27% in numeracy.

PEC was inspired by the Teaching at the Right Level (TaRL) model pioneered since the early 2000s by the Indian NGO Pratham. The TaRL model is a teaching approach that provides one-on-one assessments of students and assigns them to groups of the same learning level rather than age or grade. Students can move quickly through the groups. This way, children can progress and catch up with the expected level.

From October 2018 to June 2019, PEC was piloted in 50 primary schools. After an independent evaluation positive result, the PEC has been extended from the original 50 schools to 150 additional schools by 2020.

The PEC scaling journey to evangelize the TaRL model across Cote d'Ivoire identified four key themes:

- **Institutionalization**: Persistent focus on large-scale implementations from the start of a pilot. This ensures to foster early buy-in, identification of what is feasible and possible, and demonstration of the solution.

- **Partnerships and Collaboration**: Promote collective action with internal champions as well as external partners to bring different perspectives, resources, and expertise to drive far-reaching success and adoption.

- **Adaptation and Continuous Learning**: Integrate continuous learning to support implementation and adoption of new systems. In addition, a strong adaptive capacity to quickly respond to improvements and changes along the way of the scaling is very important while ensuring the harmonized and standardized systems are not deviating much from the original concept.

- **Costs and Financing**: Clarity on budgetary processes is very important to ensure availability and mobilization of resources for sustainable scale.

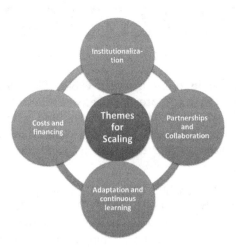

Figure P5-1. Four key themes for scaling

The preceding story has the essential themes you will need to successfully deploy employee-centric IT across your entire organization and reap all the benefits.

To help you on your journey to reaching extraordinary experience for all your employees, the next chapter, Chapter 12, will provide you the playbook you can use to deploy employee-centric IT in your organization. The playbook will be sectioned in the four key themes (institutionalization, partnerships and collaboration, adaptation and continuous learning, and costs and financing) and is the collection of all the knowledge you learned in this book, in one place.

Implementing and Scaling Employee-Centric IT for Your Company

If you have reached this chapter, it means you have joined me on the belief and journey that employee-centricity is crucial to any IT organization, and you would like now to either start implementing the concepts in this book in your organization or, if you have some of the concepts, to scale it to your entire company.

© Mark Ghibril 2023
M. Ghibril, *Employee-Centric IT*, https://doi.org/10.1007/978-1-4842-9186-3_12

Successful implementation is of course imperative for improving the outcomes of employee-centric IT as well as ensuring its long-term sustainable stability.

The purpose of this chapter is to leverage all the concepts I have mentioned in this book and act as a playbook to provide a package of key step-by-step guidance in implementing and scaling those concepts successfully. Each section will have the set of activities to be conducted and the outcomes to be expected.

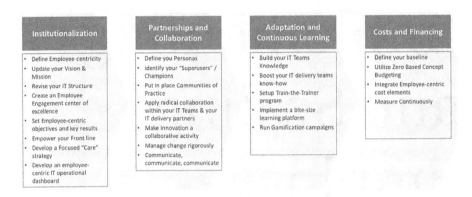

Institutionalization	Partnerships and Collaboration	Adaptation and Continuous Learning	Costs and Financing
• Define Employee-centricity • Update your Vision & Mission • Revise your IT Structure • Create an Employee Engagement center of excellence • Set Employee-centric objectives and key results • Empower your Front line • Develop a Focused "Care" strategy • Develop an employee-centric IT operational dashboard	• Define you Personas • Identify your "Superusers" / Champions • Put in place Communities of Practice • Apply radical collaboration within your IT Teams & your IT delivery partners • Make Innovation a collaborative activity • Manage change rigorously • Communicate, communicate, communicate	• Build your IT Teams Knowledge • Boost your IT delivery teams know-how • Setup Train-the-Trainer program • Implement a bite-size learning platform • Run Gamification campaigns	• Define your baseline • Utilize Zero Based Concept Budgeting • Integrate Employee-centric cost elements • Measure Continuously

Figure 12-1. Employee-centric IT playbook

Institutionalization

In the institutionalization phase, you will envision the future state and define the strategy, structure, teams, and concepts for achieving it.

To achieve extraordinary IT experience within your company, you will need to ensure your entire IT team is employee-centric and living and breathing the culture of obsession in serving the employees.

Therefore, you should start with your IT team if you like to scale employee-centricity across your entire organization.

The key activities and respective outcomes to perform are as follows:

1. **Define employee-centricity**:

    a. The outcome for this workshop is to have what employee-centricity means to your organization defined and agreed as a joint activity rather than a message from the top.

    b. How to achieve this:

        i. Run an ideation or a design thinking workshop (ideally with a facilitator whose job is to help you align and achieve the outcome) with representatives from all your IT teams, business employees, and even IT delivery partners.

    ii. Your agenda should cover

        1. Reflection on each person's experience so far within IT

        2. Why you need employee-centricity in your IT organization

        3. What employee-centric IT means

        4. What the outcomes are that can be measured to achieve employee-centricity

        5. Definition of employee-centricity

    iii. When the definition is agreed, get all your IT leadership team to be present and the workshop attendees to present to them the definition so they can ask questions and clarify any doubts, and everyone in your IT leadership team comes out of the workshop with full commitment that they understand what employee-centricity means to their teams and their area of responsibility.

2. **Update your vision and mission:**

    a. The outcome for this step is to reflect the importance of employee-centricity in your IT vision and mission, and the entire IT organization understands the importance of being obsessed with serving the employees.

    b. How to achieve this:

        i. Take the definition from your workshop and try to add the keywords from the definition as well as the word "employee-centricity" to your vision and mission.

        ii. Communicate this to your entire IT organization in a town hall, ask your IT leaders to reiterate the same message in their teams, and answer any clarification questions.

        iii. Communicate the importance of employee-centricity in IT to the rest of the organization.

3. **Revise your IT structure**:

    a. The outcome for this step is to have all teams driving toward employee-centricity in the same direction, and each IT team member understands their contribution to the employee-centric vision.

    b. How to achieve this:

        i. Revisit your IT structure and adopt a functional employee-centric setup that should have at least the following criteria:

            1. Functional teams consist of cross-departmental team members with the full end-to-end accountability toward the employees for specific IT products they use in their daily processes.

        ii. Don't completely change your current organizational setup (i.e., HR-related setup) as this will cause way more disruption than help; unless you are running an entire transformation within your organization, then I suggest you combine both.

        iii. Just keep in mind:

            1. The above and everything concerning the employees' daily activities in a certain process/business area can be tackled within one functional team while organizational teams keep improving on quality and costs of your IT organization.

4. **Create an employee engagement center of excellence**:

    a. The outcome is to have high-quality, standardized, and cross-IT product experience to the entire organization when they interact with IT.

    b. How to achieve this:

        i. Set up a small team consisting of multidisciplinary team members (a mix of IT and non-IT backgrounds) that regularly assess the employee-centricity maturity of your entire organization, collect feedback from your employees, and work with each of your organizational and functional teams to drive improvements and increase the level of employee experience.

    ii. Empower this team to have full power to stop activities that are not driving the right outcome that aligns with your employee-centric vision.

    iii. Ensure your IT employees who are in the center of excellence are also part of the functional teams to help always drive the "voice of the employee" in case it is forgotten or missed.

    iv. The charter of the employee engagement center of excellence can cover the following:

        1. Developing employee interaction, readiness, and adoption methods and concepts to enhance engagement

        2. Managing IT/digital training, roadshows, and events to be used across your organization

        3. Developing IT satisfaction concepts to measure, analyze, and improve employees' satisfaction with IT.

        4. Developing communities of practice concepts

5. **Set employee-centric objectives and key results:**

  a. The outcome is to have employee-centric attitudes and results from your IT employees.

  b. How to achieve it:

    i. Add to your performance measurement process both subjective and objective targets that instill employee-centric attitudes and results for all your IT employees.

    ii. Subjective targets should be based on a set of employee-centric attitudes you expect from all your IT employees, such as

        1. Listening

        2. Caring

        3. Communication

        4. Collaboration

           iii. Objective targets should be based on end-to-end outcomes for the employees rather than purely personal, isolated targets, such as

              1. Increased employee satisfaction

              2. Reduced number of IT incidents

6. **Empower your front line**:

    a. The outcome is to have your frontline IT team members (including your IT delivery partners) who directly and regularly interact with employees across the organization able to make decisions that provide the employee an extraordinary IT experience.

    b. How to achieve this:

        i. Empower your agents and IT support staff to own the employees' issues (end to end) and have the power to get the right support from your IT organization to resolve the topics quickly.

        1. Each IT agent owns all the tickets in their queues and is empowered to force and chase other levels in the organization to resolve the ticket to the employee's expectations.

        ii. Train and elevate the knowledge of your frontline IT staff so they feel comfortable that they can own the issues but also respond in the right level of urgency.

           1. Train your agents on listening and building a personal level of interaction.

           2. Rerun this training program every six months at the beginning and adapt it as you learn what is working and what needs improvement.

        iii. Be sure to communicate this ownership and empowerment to the rest of your IT teams.

7. **Develop a focused "care" strategy**:

    a. The outcome is clear channels of engagement and support for employees to engage easily and simply with IT and take into consideration the problem complexities and communicate them.

b. How to achieve this:

    i. Set up a self-service channel such as a portal where employees can get knowledge articles, order IT equipment, or raise their special demands through. Here, the quality of content and the channel are important to succeed.

    ii. Set up a crowdsourcing service such as a social network group where employees can engage with IT and other colleagues to get help for simple problems and clarification questions or get best practice examples in using certain functionalities. Here, the responsiveness from your IT teams toward the posts is crucial to make this channel trusted by the employees.

    iii. Set up an assisted channel such as a community of practice on a specific product and there ensure the right IT experts or employee champions are available to answer the more complicated problems/topics.

    iv. Set up a personal service which offers chat, phone, and virtual/physical drop-in centers that facilitate one-on-one communications with employees to listen to their complex issues.

8. **Develop an employee-centric IT Operations dashboard**:

    a. The outcome is to allow you to measure and show your progress toward your employee-centricity vision and offer full transparency to your organization on that journey.

    b. How to achieve this:

        i. Create an online dashboard that includes easy-to-understand and transparent key performance indicators that you believe your employees require to see. Some suggestions are as follows:

            1. Health of your applications and networks

            2. Major incidents and actions

            3. Gamification campaigns and improvement actions underway

            4. Restrictions currently in place due to certain issues

ii. Allow your data to be filtered on department and country levels.

iii. Ensure that all your personas can benefit from the data shared.

iv. Include both qualitative and quantitative data.

By completing this phase, you have set up the right foundations for employee-centricity to allow your IT teams to relentlessly focus on delivery toward that goal and sustainably scale the experience to your entire organization. From here, you will need to jump into building the right collaboration and partnership. That will be covered in the next section.

Partnerships and Collaboration

In the partnerships and collaboration phase, you will build the ecosystem that brings the employee-centric culture to be lived by your IT teams and experienced by your employees.

The ecosystem will succeed if you correctly define your communities, collaboration triggers, communication strategy, and change management.

The key activities and respective outcomes to perform are as follows:

1. **Define your personas**:

   1. The outcome is to strengthen the focus on employee-centricity by understanding better who IT is serving and enabling within their organization.

   2. How to achieve this:

      - Define personas that are concrete and include their IT literacy and expectations.

      - Make it simple and transparent that everyone in IT can understand them and apply them to their area of expertise.

      - Perform a simple assessment in how many of your employees fit in each of the personas (start with assumptions).

      - Reconfirm these numbers as you run your IT satisfaction surveys by clearly asking employees certain questions that identify which persona they are.

2. **Identify your "superusers"/champions:**

   1. The outcome is to build a group of change agents and ambassadors in the business that works closely with IT and be multipliers within their departments, locations, and businesses.

   2. How to achieve this:

      • Utilize your personas to identify the employees that could be the right potential.

      • Let your IT leadership work with business leadership to understand the benefit of those "superusers" and the need of dedicated time to engage with IT. I recommend formalizing their activities as superusers as well in their target settings to keep their motivation to the activities and role.

      • Engage them early with all your IT activities and let them feel their voice is heard from the feedback they provide to the importance of their role.

3. **Put in place communities of practice:**

   1. The outcome is a space for collective engagement on IT topics (either generic or specialized) to improve productivity and the use of digital tools and increase employee experience with their daily IT.

   2. How to achieve this:

      • Set up for each of your IT products a community of superusers/champions that allows them to engage directly with your IT experts.

      • Ensure the moderation of that community is done by IT to drive the right discussions that benefit your employee-centric vision. If such communities exist within the business, then join them, listen, and drive engagement as well.

4. **Apply radical collaboration within your IT teams and your IT delivery partners:**

   1. The outcome is to achieve a strong sense of ownership and joint teamwork in achieving employee-centric environment across the end-to-end IT value chain.

2. How to achieve this:

- You should instill these simple principles across your IT teams and with your IT delivery partners:

- Employee-centricity is a responsibility of everyone, not any one team.

- Collaboration means debate and time should be taken to discuss, challenge, and come up with employee-centric solutions.

- If a team can't agree, that's OK; take it next level up for decision.

- With the preceding principles, everyone can feel empowered and encouraged to collaborate to succeed and achieve employee-centric outcomes, irrespective of their role.

5. **Make innovation a collaborative activity:**

1. The outcome is to create a culture of creative thought and drive across your entire organization when it is related to IT.

2. How to achieve this:

- Provide the space and time for your IT teams to think. I suggest you allow 10% to 20% of your team member's time to be freed up from day-to-day work.

- Instill the culture of "collaborative innovation" supporting and nudging your team to collaborate with each other and with other departments and IT delivery partners on problems the employees are facing or insights that need to be tackled.

- If you have a major challenge to solve, don't leave it to the 10% time of your employees, dedicate the right resources for 100% of the time to tackle it quickly and efficiently.

- Ensure your team knows that incremental innovation is as important (if not more) as radical innovation, and therefore every step of improvement is a success.

- Run a hackathon once a year to drive parallel concepts to a large challenge, while run as many ideation workshops as you need.

6. **Manage change rigorously**:

    1. The outcome is for employees to be aware and acknowledge the change you are driving (big or small) and are able to understand its impact, benefits and able to feel comfortable to work effectively during and after it is completed.

    2. How to achieve this:

        • Define and oversee a change management framework that works for you. Utilize one of the concepts available and adapt it to your needs (don't reinvent the wheel).

        • Provide a centralized group of experts that can support all IT teams and programs with the change. You can combine this group under the employee engagement center of excellence as this fits well from talent and direction.

        • Instill ownership of change management on project managers and IT leaders and not purely on the expert group. They should be used purely as consultants/executors, but ownership always is with the change instigators.

        • Provide enough resources and time to dedicate to the change management activities. In my experience, all stakeholders (business and IT) involved in a project or program should dedicate at least 20% of their time to change management if they want to succeed.

        • Execute a thorough stakeholder analysis at the beginning of your project/transformation while reviewing it with every milestone to update it/improve it.

        • Put in place a community of insiders and superusers who will be your change agents that can facilitate the change process, distribute knowledge by ensuring those who get stuck get the help they need, and ensure collective energy is spent toward the transformation journey.

        • Run a change impact analysis with all stakeholders as early as possible. Ensure to include your community of insiders and superusers in those sessions. Some sessions will be quick and easy, and others will need workshops to share the target tools and processes and identify the change impact and gaps from today's as-is situation. Don't skip this step, ever, and cover

- Processes

- Tools/technology

- People/network

- Utilize methods such as design thinking to ensure all impacted employees are involved as well as understanding the different roles and stages employees might be at during the change life cycle.

7. **Communicate, communicate, communicate**:

1. The outcome is to have an effective reach and understanding in your IT communications that touch the hearts and minds of your employees and have the right impact and understanding across your entire organization.

2. How to achieve this:

- Identify with your corporate communications teams as well as focus group from your business employees what style of communications fit your company culture.

- Don't constrain yourself to one style; however, it is good to understand the different styles that could exist and ensure your communication covers them all.

- As a general rule of thumb, your communication style should

- Cover directive and advice-oriented elements to reach everyone

- Cover individualistic and collectivist reasoning of the benefits of your request

- Have a clear context that provides a clear direction but leaves space for all to take what fits their cultures

- Deliver your communications across mixed channels and media (e.g., written, video, audio, face-to-face).

- Deliver frequent communications and stick to that frequency as employees' expectations will be set.

- Get IT and business leaders to reiterate a summary of those communications in town halls and department meetings, as employees trust and listen most to their direct supervisors and leaders.

When you complete this phase, you have catalyzed a collective action and fostered close collaboration, partnership, and an alliance with your business and IT delivery partners. Through the superusers and champions and your IT teams, you created the right conditions, mindset shift, and behavior change to drive employee-centricity in scale across all IT activities, transformation, and operations. From here, you will need to jump into building the right collaboration and partnership. That will be covered in the next section.

Adaptation and Continuous Learning

In the adaptation and continuous learning phase, you will develop a continuous learning culture, strengthen your adaptive capacity to change, and ensure there is time and resources for learning, exchange, and feedback.

The key activities and respective outcomes to perform are as follows:

1. **Build your IT team's knowledge:**

   a. The outcome is a well-versed and knowledgeable IT workforce that is consistently listening to your employees, aware of IT's impact on the organization, and producing extraordinary experience.

   b. How to achieve this:

      i. All levels of your IT organization must possess the same obsession about employee-centricity.

      ii. Run an "employee-centricity @ IT" training program that provides key skills and knowledge you expect from your entire IT team. The following are just a sample of what to include:

1. Skills

    a. Emotional intelligence with specific emphasis on listening, empathy, and caring

    b. Communication with emphasis on context and style

    c. Collaboration with emphasis on cross-team and cross-culture engagement

    d. Critical thinking and cognitive flexibility with emphasis on dealing with change

2. Knowledge

    a. Cross-department knowledge to understand the end-to-end processes that employees go through as well as the role each of their IT team members delivers

    b. Ideation/design thinking frameworks and how to apply them effectively

    c. Change management frameworks and key steps

    d. Persona development and utilization

    e. Employee journey maps to be able to visualize end-to-end interactions

    f. Data mining especially for IT satisfaction surveys

iii. Rerun this training program every six months at the beginning and adapt it as you learn what is working and what needs improvement.

iv. Train all your IT leaders on motivational interviewing and coaching and consistently reemphasize this skill within your succession planning.

v. In all your IT town halls and department meetings, ensure employee-centric KPIs are shared and discussed. This includes but is not limited to

    1. IT satisfaction results

    2. IT tickets/incident volumes

    3. Major incidents

4. Feedback summary from employees

vi. If you have screens across your office, continuously display those KPIs.

2. **Boost your IT delivery team's know-how**:

a. The outcome is anyone involved in IT delivery delivers the high-level employee-centric care and outcomes.

b. How to achieve this:

i. For your key IT delivery partners (those who are involved in your major programs/projects or your daily operations), mandate that their employees go through your "employee-centricity @ IT" training program.

ii. Ensure they have regular access to all IT satisfaction results and other employee-centricity KPIs.

3. **Set up a train-the-trainer program**:

a. The outcome is strong, knowledgeable superusers which regularly refresh and disseminate the knowledge IT tools and processes to the entire organization.

b. How to achieve this:

i. Define a train-the-trainer program that is formal and available within your organization learning and development structure. This gives it formality and makes superusers more interested to take part.

ii. Set up two structures for such programs:

1. **Project Structure**: This is the training that will be provided to superusers during a project/transformation program.

2. **Business As Usual Structure**: This is the continuous training to be provided to superusers to keep their knowledge refreshed.

      iii. In project mode

         1. Training superusers should be conducted by knowledgeable IT trainers that can provide the technical knowledge and can respond to any questions superusers have. These trainers should be also accessible during the project in case questions come up from the superusers.

         2. Superusers should conduct intensive training sessions to the employees ahead of the release of the new functionality or tool.

      iv. In business as usual mode

         1. Offer all content on an online repository with bite-sized content that can be utilized by both superusers and employees.

         2. Onboarding of new superusers or employees should be provided in a two-step approach:

            a. Self-learning at first using the online repository

            b. Question and answer session with a superuser to clarify any questions they might have

4. Implement a bite-sized learning platform:

  a. The outcome is the easy and simple access to required information and knowledge to keep continuous learning for all your organization on IT-related topics.

  b. How to achieve this:

      i. Implement a bite-sized learning platform with the following characteristics:

         1. Ability to store short, specialized content on any IT topic, tool, or process

         2. Ability to easily update and refresh content

         3. Ability to search very easily across an entire platform

         4. Ability to store all types of content (e.g., video, audio, slides)

5. Ability to set "learning paths" depending on the personas, roles, department, and other characteristics you might need

6. Ability to measure the progress on each of those content and learning paths

ii. Train your IT teams, IT delivery partners, and superusers regularly on this learning platform as they will be your key content creators, and without great content, your platform will not be used by the rest of your organization.

iii. If needed, supplement your bite-sized learning platform with adoption tools that can integrate with your tools directly and provide on-screen steps.

5. **Run gamification campaigns:**

a. The outcome is engaging learning and education that is continuous, exciting, and employee-centric.

b. How to achieve this:

i. Start by defining the business goals you want to achieve. I suggest not to exceed three business goals at the same time.

ii. Identify the target areas your employees are struggling with in relation to

1. Their behavior toward IT. Again, to ensure focused outcomes, choose one behavior to achieve per business goal.

2. Identify the impact you are seeking on both short and long terms.

3. Prioritize the individual-level mechanics and develop to group or collective as you mature.

4. Apply concepts that include

a. Points and badges

b. Levels and ratings

c. Recognition points and interactions

5. Don't overengineer your gamification solution. Pilot an out-of-the-box solution from the market and only develop your own if you are confident that you have a culture that supports gamification and you tested it and succeeded from your pilot/minimum viable product (MVP).

iii. At all stages, keep the data flowing effectively and transparently to your entire organization as part of your employee-centric IT operations dashboard.

iv. Integrate your gamification data into your prioritization mechanism for your IT team's tasks and activities.

As you complete this phase, you have integrated a continuous learning culture within your organization supporting implementations, adaptations, and course corrections along the way. Now let's jump into the last phase, which is all about ensuring you are executing effectively and winning the buy-in from your organization on the investment and financing needed for your employee-centric IT journey.

Costs and Financing

In the costs and financing phase, you will prepare your financing for employee-centricity in your IT organization, ensure there is clarity on what is needed to mobilize the resources, and ensure you have the sound cost projections as you scale your implementations.

The key activities and respective outcomes to perform are as follows:

1. **Define your baseline**:

   a. The outcome is a transparent and clear baseline of your IT costs before you set off on the employee-centric journey.

   b. How to achieve this:

   i. As traditional IT budgeting is fairly consistent year over year, identify the operational and investment costs in your IT organization.

ii. Identify any budgets/costs you have in your baseline covering employee-centric concepts mentioned previously. This is analyzing the budgets you currently spend on

    1. Change management

    2. Communication

    3. Collaboration

    4. Training and education

    5. Employee and community engagement

    6. IT support

    7. Innovation

2. **Utilize zero-based concept budgeting:**

a. The outcome is a budget for the employee-centric IT that is based on your "future" needs rather than on your past experiences.

b. How to achieve this:

    i. Utilize the zero-based concepts (ZBC) to plan your budget for the upcoming year based on your employee-centric strategy rather than based on the previous budget.

    ii. Define your "zero" which is the lean, simple, and minimum investment you need to operate and transform IT without employee-centric activities.

    iii. Define your North Star which is the ideal target to achieve your full employee-centric IT organization with all the investments needed to achieve the concepts mentioned in this book.

    iv. Set a defined time you like to achieve it (speed of implementation depends on the current state of your organization). The following triggers in your organization can be used as excellent vehicles to speed up your implementation significantly:

        1. A merger, acquisition, or a carve-out

        2. Transformative change programs

3. **Integrate employee-centric cost elements**:

   a. The outcome is clear cost elements and financing in place for employee-centric activities in your operational and transformational activities.

   b. How to achieve this:

      i. Ensure your budgets and costs always reflect transparently the employee-centric costs.

      ii. These cost elements are (but not restricted to) as follows:

         1. Operational cost elements

            a. Training budgets for train-the-trainer and employee-centric care programs

            b. Percentage of time you will need from your entire IT workforce to spend more on to live employee-centric culture

            c. Employee engagement experience center resources and activities (such as roadshows)

            d. Learning platforms and the content that is required to be created

            e. Communication activities (including design) for continuous communications

            f. Skills development and IT leader motivational speaking and coaching trainings

         2. Transformational cost elements

            a. Change management costs covering resources, training, and content creation and distribution

4. **Measure continuously**:

   a. The outcome is a tracked outcome of investments related to employee-centricity.

   b. How to achieve this:

      i. Even though tracking employee-centricity is related to employee happiness, employee engagement, and employee retention, additional metrics can be measured.

ii.   Some of these metrics are as follows:

1. **Productivity**: You can compare time spent by your employees on IT-related issues or information searching before you implemented your employee-centric organization to after it.

2. **Onboarding Speed**: You can identify the quality and speed of onboarding of new employees before and after employee-centricity has been ingrained in your IT teams.

3. **IT Satisfaction**: You can quickly reflect the impact of your employee-centric investments on the satisfaction of your employees.

Employee-centric costs and funding are an iterative process that continuously needs to be measured and improved, and the value from it will not only be seen within the IT organization but across the entire organization.

Conclusion: There Is No End in Sight

If you have made it so far, I believe you have achieved and acquired enough knowledge that will empower you to drive employee-centricity in your IT and digital teams. You will automatically increase your overall productivity and efficiency and drive business value within the company and ultimately toward your customers.

Businesses in this digital age face fierce competition and unprecedented uncertainty and velocity. Hence, changeability for organizations and individuals alike is no longer "nice to have" but a "must-have." With that change, every part of the organization, especially IT, the digital backbone, has to support that change.

A McKinsey survey has shown that 60% of employees are unsatisfied with the technology companies provide them to do their work. Given the high cost of recruiting new employees and the significant amount of employee turnover in this digital age, companies must consider how technology might help them improve their ability to attract and retain their workers. Here, IT comes into play and why employee-centric IT is a must-have.

© Mark Ghibril 2023
M. Ghibril, *Employee-Centric IT*, https://doi.org/10.1007/978-1-4842-9186-3

By winning the hearts and minds of your employees, IT becomes a creative, innovative, and value-driven organization that the rest of the business can rely on to thrive to digital mastery and execution.

In this digital era, where hyper-change is being seen in all areas of the personal and professional lives, there will be no end destination when it comes to digital transformation. It will be a continuous cycle of improvement upon improvement. The ideas and learnings from this book are just the beginning, and I am confident everyone can continuously improve on these ideas.

I hope you apply the learnings from this book and improvement, and I am looking forward to hearing your learnings and new ideas. My hope is that the topic of employee-centricity becomes ingrained in all IT organizations around the world in the near future.

Index

© Mark Ghibril 2023
M. Ghibril, *Employee-Centric IT*, https://doi.org/10.1007/978-1-4842-9186-3